DOING
BUSINESS
IN
CHINA

"Doing Business in China—The Sun Tzu's Way" provides valuable insight for those looking to succeed in China. Laurence Brahm has put his years of experience into an easy-to-read book that will serve as a valuable tool for anyone entering the world's most complex and fastest growing market."
—*Scott Kronick, Managing Director, Ogilvy Public Relations Worldwide, China*

"... one of the few indispensable books anyone attempting to negotiate business deals in China must read; and Brahm is a China hand who knows the territory... To ignore it would be like going into battle unarmed."
—*Mike Furst, Senior Vice President, The Balloch Group*

"Laurence Brahm, himself a successful businessman in Beijing, has produced a practical guide to doing business in China.... While Brahm focuses on the complexities of negotiation for new entrants in the market, this book is equally useful in applying Sun Tzu's precepts to business in general for all who seek to be successful in the complex and dynamic China market."
—*Michael T. Byrnes, Chief Representative, Rockwell China*

"An enjoyable read about the rigors of negotiating deals in China...filled with valuable lessons for prospective investors."
—*Jon Eichelberger, Partner, Perkins Coie LLP, Beijing Office*

"Very enlightening... an indispensable reference to doing business in the PRC."
—*Kin-Seng Lai, Vice-President, Petroleum Marketing,*
ExxonMobil China Petroleum & Petrochemical Company Limited

Laurence J. Brahm is a political economist and lawyer by profession, residing in Beijing. He has served as a government advisor on China's state owned enterprise, restructuring financial and most recent media reforms.

Author of over twenty books on China, including *When Yes Means No, China's Century*, and *China as No. 1*, he is a recognized international, media commentator on developments in the country.

As individual entrepreneur, he founded Red Capital Studio and today spends most of his time pioneering alternative multi-media productions on China. He has also restored a number of historic ancient courtyards in Beijing which include the celebrated Red Capital club and boutique luxury hotels.

After spending two decades negotiating investments in China for major multinational corporations, Laurence Brahm finally became completely fed up. He no longer works as a lawyer and consultant. After reading this book one will understand why.

DOING BUSINESS
IN
CHINA

The Sun Tzu Way

Laurence J. Brahm

TUTTLE PUBLISHING
Boston • Rutland, Vermont • Tokyo

Published by Tuttle Publishing, an imprint of Periplus Editions (HK) Ltd, with editiorial offices at 130 Joo Seng Road, #06-01/03, Singapore 368357, and 153 Milk Street, Boston, Massachusetts 02109

ISBN 0-8048-3531-4

Printed in Singapore

Distributed by:

North America, Latin America and Europe
Tuttle Publishing
Airport Industrial Park, 364 Innovation Drive,
North Clarendon, VT 05759-9436
Tel: (802) 773 8930
Fax: (802) 773 6993
Email: info@tuttlepublishing.com
www.tuttlepublishing.com

Japan
Tuttle Publishing
Yaekari Building, 3F
5-4-12 Osaki, Shinagawa-ku
Tokyo 141-0032
Tel: (813) 5437 0171
Fax: (813) 5437 0755
Email: tuttle-sales@gol.com

Asia Pacific
Berkeley Books Pte Ltd
130 Joo Seng Road, #06-01/03
Singapore 368357
Tel: (65) 6280 1330
Fax: (65) 6280 6290
Email: inquiries@periplus.com.sg

08 07 06 05 04
8 7 6 5 4 3 2 1

Contents

PART **1**

Sun Tzu's Art of Negotiating

Appendices

Glossary   157

FOREWORD

When doing business in China, one faces more than the cultural barriers of picking up peanuts with chopsticks. Vast differences in perceptions and cultural collective sub-conscious are most definitively clear when "friendship" propaganda touted by Chinese officialdom develops into real relationships, especially business ones.

No wonder the Chinese read Sun Tzu repeatedly from childhood. The master strategist's text applies to situations ranging from business and personal relations to romance. Foreign businessmen wishing to enter the China market to stay and survive should heed his words.

Businessmen traveling regularly to China often find "second wives" or concubines. This long tradition, briefly wiped out under communism, has revived. China's communists today are more capitalist than the capitalists going there to do business. Concubine popularity now grows faster than China's GDP.

One Hong Kong businessman fell in love with a gorgeous girl from Sichuan, brought her to Beijing and rented an apartment. Colleagues warned about potential risks inherent in such arrangements. He laughed assuring the situation was under control. Such a nice girl would patiently wait for him to visit Beijing each week.

Then she wanted gifts from Hong Kong, beginning with expensive handbags, jewelry, Swiss watches, and later, a Lexus. The Hong Kong businessman then realized that long-term concubine maintenance was a costly proposition. Enough! Informing the landlord, he finished the rental agreement at month's end, informing his lovely concubine. She batted her eyelids in surprise, but responded in a soft, sweet voice, "That's alright. I understand."

But when vacating the apartment, she stopped up the drains in the bathroom sink, shower, bathtub, and kitchen. She then turned on all the taps, locked the door behind her, and threw away the key. She disappeared into the vast province of Sichuan.

Two days later four apartments below were destroyed by ceiling and wall leaks and horrendous water damage. Police investigating the suspected water source smashed down the locked doors only to get washed by a small flood. The Hong Kong owner was traced and his Beijing office had to compensate five apartment owners for damages suffered. The Hong Kong businessman was fired.

This story provides a very specific lesson concerning the risks of doing business in China and, an important moral lesson —the girls in Sichuan are very pretty, but they are not stupid. Moreover, the Hong Kong businessman should have read Sun Tzu first.

Finding the Man
with the Key

"The man with the key is not here," explained the drably dressed hotel business centre attendant with the simple bob-cut hair.

"What? Do you know how many times I have heard this in China—'the man with the key is not here'—I've had it," screamed the executive.

"But I am most terribly and sincerely sorry to you. But the man with the key is not here."

"Then, where the hell is he?"

"He must have gone away."

"I know he went away. That's why I am screaming at you. Where is he?"

"He must be somewhere."

"Where?!"

"He must be resting. It is resting time now. Maybe he went home. Maybe he will come back tomorrow."

"I need him here today—now! The conference room is locked in your hotel's stupid business center and my computer and papers are all there. I need them, and I need them now!"

"You can come back tomorrow when the man with the key comes back," suggested the attendant with a dim smile.

"I can't come back later. I need those papers now. I have to call long distance and discuss important business."

"It is OK. It is late now and the people you may call may need to rest too. I think maybe you just wait until tomorrow when the man with the key returns."

"That's ridiculous. People aren't resting. It is the middle of the working day in Europe."

"Maybe you need a rest too."

"I need my computer and the papers. I need them now!"

"But tomorrow the man with the key will come back and...."

"No! I am checking out of this hotel first thing tomorrow morning and leaving. I need my computer, my papers and everything else I left in that conference room. Anyway, my credit card is there with my things and I need it to pay the hotel bill tomorrow."

"It's OK. You can pay with cash. We prefer cash."

"No! I have to leave for an early flight tomorrow. I cannot miss my flight."

"It's OK. If you miss your flight, no worries. There are lots of nice sights to see in our city. If you have not seen them, you should see them all!"

INTRODUCTION
A Day in the Life of a Negotiator

Afternoon

They had been there for a week. The conference room of the hotel business center was piled high with papers and dirty coffee cups. It was as if all the negotiators had been camping out in the room. In fact, to some extent they had.

Tick-tick-tick… The foreign side's Hong Kong secretary was meticulously tapping all of the minutes of the negotiation into her laptop computer fearing she would miss a detail.

On the Chinese side, the minute-taker was scratching every detail into his notebook with a pen. The foreign side's lawyer sat poised, staring at all of the contract papers sprawled on the table before him and thinking of all of the billable hours he would be able to squeeze from sorting out the clerical mess. The Chinese side's lawyer was reading a newspaper.

The financial adviser on the foreign side whispered some details into the foreign chief negotiator's ears. "I think you will have to cancel your airline ticket again," he counseled. "Can they get me a first-class ticket for this weekend?" the chief negotiator for the foreign side whispered back. His financial advisor was silent. "Business class?" More silence. "I refuse to fly economy again..." snapped the foreign chief negotiator. Someone on the Chinese side burped.

The pressure between the two key negotiators representing the Chinese and foreign side respectively, had been building up all week. The pressure on both chief negotiators was as heavy as the social burden of a State-owned enterprise.

Each side had to meet deadlines. Each had to make strategic gains for his enterprise with this round of negotiations. Both sides had to gain some advantage. It was time for each side to move, to take initiative—now!

Smoke from cigarettes whirled upwards from ashtrays like miniature incense burners. Someone on the Chinese side cut the silence with the whisk of a match. Both chief negotiators cracked.

Dusk

"This is ridiculous," screamed the foreign chief negotiator. "We are bringing so much into your community by way of investment and you won't cooperate with any of our ideas. What's wrong with you?"

"You foreigners think you are so almighty that you do not have to obey our laws or respect our customs," the Chinese chief negotiator screamed back.

"Don't you realize what we are doing for you? We are investing in your little pit of a community. We are going to save your State-owned enterprise from collapse. Without our money you will be nothing. And here you are throwing it away for being stubborn," retorted the foreign negotiator. "You have no respect for the Chinese system. You have no respect for Chinese law. You have no understanding of our special situation in China," snapped his Chinese counterpart.

Meanwhile, the translator from the Chinese side and the translator from the foreign side stood up and walked out of the negotiation room. They had refused to translate any of the tart words thrown between the two parties. They stood in the hallway outside the negotiation room and had a cigarette together. In fact, they ended up smoking a whole pack.

"What's wrong with you? Don't you want our investment? Do you want us to take our investment somewhere else?" screamed the foreign negotiatior.

"You do not understand our country. You do not understand our system. You do not care about our country. You do not care about our people," yelled the Chinese negotiator.

"We will take our investment elsewhere. Don't think that we won't. We've had it. Why should we invest if we can't have the terms we want?" retorted the foreign negotiator.

"You do not respect our laws. You insist on always following your rules. But you are in China. China has China's rules. You must obey China's rules in China."

"So you are going to let our investment go elsewhere? What's wrong with you? Are you stupid? You must be stupid. We are about to invest all this money and all you can do is think of creating more problems. Well, we will take our money and go elsewhere!"

"You are forcing unequal terms on China. This contract is an unequal treaty. You are an imperialist. All of you foreigners have AIDS!"

The discussion continued inside the room, but as nobody was translating, neither of the negotiation team leaders could understand what the other was saying. So each screamed louder in order to be heard better to compensate for the fact that both spoke different languages, and neither could communicate with the other.

Night

When the translators had finished their pack of cigarettes, they returned to the negotiation room. By this time, everybody was very excitable because nobody understood what the other was saying and everybody was trying to make a point.

Both chief negotiators had sore throats. The two translators suggested that they break for the day and go out to Hard Rock Café as a group, so as to calm down relations between the two.

Both sides went to the café. Everybody had a nice time and all of the animosity thrown around the negotiation room that day was forgotten. Both chief negotiators got drunk and even danced together. Everything was alright. Neither had understood what the other had said that day, anyway.

Morning

The next day, the negotiation started late because everybody had slept in after the exhausting day of negotiations and evening of fun and frivolity. The Chinese side opened the negotiations.

"Do you know that the Western food we ate last night tasted terrible? We cannot stand eating Western food. Chinese food is much better," complained the chief negotiator on the Chinese side.

"So you expect us to eat Chinese food every day just because we are in China? Forget it!"

"Sorry. You are in China. The future joint venture will only have a Chinese food canteen," explained the Chinese negotiator.

"The future joint venture will have to have a Western food canteen. We will insist upon this," the foreign chief negotiator lashed back.

"It cannot. Our employees only know how to cook Chinese food."

"We will bring in an expatriate chef."

"We won't accept that. He will cost too much money. We have enough foreign expatriate managers. Their salary is eating up the profits of the joint venture. We refuse to allow any more!"

"I suggest we have another cigarette," the translator called to his counterpart across the table.

"I agree," replied the counterpart. "Let's go...."

PART I
Sun Tzu's Art of Negotiating

*"Master, what is one to do when they are
frustrated in prolonged negotiations?"*

*"Grasshopper, patience is a virtue.
It has the effect of water dripping on a stone."*

*"But Master, what if the
water is dripping on sand?"*

Getting Started

"He who knows the art of the direct and the indirect
approach will be victorious. Such is the art of maneuvering"

—SUN TZU

"Yes" in China may be the first word of agreement, but is not always the last word in negotiations. "Yes" is often simply another way of saying, "Let's begin to talk seriously." The Chinese often interpret the conclusion of a contract to mean that the two parties now understand each other well enough to begin asking for further favors.

What may be viewed as simply a favor to one party may seem like a costly concession to the other. For the Western party, a contract is a contract and the obligations of the parties are those obligations spelled out therein. Western culture is goal-oriented. Negotiations are simply a process through which the final goal—the contract—is reached.

Chinese society is process-oriented. Consequently, their negotiations often involve understandings and intentions which are not spelled out in the final contract. These can resurface at any time, often couched in phrases like "Based on our friendship and mutual understanding, could you please...."

Because of Confucian values and the Chinese emphasis on interpersonal relations, these requests may have nothing to do with the contract terms at all, and can range from things like "Can you get my kid into an American college to study?" to "Our company/factory would like a new Mercedes Benz."

Despite the emphasis on interpersonal relations, the Chinese are tough negotiators. Western businessmen often find contract negotiations in China to be a traumatic and stressful endurance test. Chinese negotiating tactics have been best described as being analogous to guerrilla warfare: "Strike hard, retreat, seize a position, reject compromise, and strike again."

Should it be surprising that such tactics are used? Strategic philosophy has a long history in China. Chinese leaders, both political and military, from Cao Cao of the Three Kingdoms Period to Mao Zedong of modern times, have looked to a Machiavellian philosophy recorded by Sun Wu (known to the world as "Sun Tzu" or "Master Sun") in his treatise, *Art of War*, more than 2,000 years ago.

In a sense, SunTzu's *Art of War*, like other writings from China's classical period, has worked its way into the collective subconscious of Chinese diplomatic thinking. It is not hard to see how the strategies propounded by Sun Tzu are directly applicable to the negotiating style characterized by China's negotiators today.

The Strategical Attack

"Keep him under strain and wear him down."

—SUN TZU

For the Western business person, a negotiation in China may seem like a protracted guerrilla warfare. This is because the Chinese use every possible psychological and physiological ploy to wear down the opposing party. As Sun Tzu wrote, "Attack where he is unprepared; sally out where he does not expect you." In negotiations, this is precisely what the Chinese do.

It is often suggested that Western negotiators should be careful about the amount of tea they drink during negotiations because discussions often drag on for hours without a break. While Western negotiations often include planned breaks, the Chinese see negotiations as a means of testing the opposition's resolve.

When coming to China for negotiations, Western business-men should abandon their MBA textbooks and heed Sun Tzu's advice that "invincibility depends on one's self; the enemy's vulnerability on himself." It follows that "those skilled ... can make themselves invincible but cannot cause an enemy to be ... vulnerable."

One should not forget the mistake of one British negotiator who made himself vulnerable by agreeing to remain in China and continue discussions over the Christmas holidays. He should have read Sun Tzu. The Chinese had. They knew that the Christmas period would greatly reduce their opponent's resistance to pressure for concessions.

Whenever the Chinese side knows that foreign negotiators are working against deadlines, they will begin to protract the negotiations for as long as possible. If the foreign negotiators are in a remote factory, they will delay work with long drawn out lunches, excessive drinking and will afterwards sleep or go to the sauna, leaving half the day wasted until the evening when such revelry begins again.

On one hand, this may be seen as delaying tactics. On the other, it is a way to know the foreign partner in different moods and situations. The Chinese do not think of business as business and friendship as friendship. Rather, they see everything as mixed together. This difference in perception creates acute problems not only in the negotiation stage, but ever more so in the operations stage. Once they begin, the Chinese management will want to introduce friends and relatives to work alongside foreign professionals who have been assigned to tasks. Eventually, new negotiations will need to be held to resolve these problems too.

It is not surprising that increasing numbers of multi-nationals are closing down joint ventures, buying out their Chinese partners and establishing wholly foreign owned entities, or selling their equity and leaving altogether. Everyone has their limitations.

Opening Negotiations

"Ground which both we and the enemy can traverse with equal ease is called accessible. In such ground, he who first takes high sunny positions can fight advantageously."

—SUN TZU

The Chinese open negotiations by trying to establish their own ground rules. They do this by pressing their foreign counterparts to agree to certain general principles. The agreement to such principles usually takes the form of a "letter of intent." To the Westerner, these principles may seem like ritual statements because they lack any kind of specific detail.

Be careful. One should not make too many assumptions regarding initial formalities. As Chang Yu wrote in his commentary on the *Art of War*, "If one should be the first to occupy a position on level ground, how much does this apply to difficult and dangerous places?"

The Chinese understand this well. The principles initially agreed to will set up a conceptual parameter within which the parties must work in order for discussions to progress. Later, the Chinese may invoke these principles to suggest that the foreign party has not lived up to the spirit of "mutual cooperation and benefit" initially agreed upon.

The Chinese emphasis on general principles strikes an unusual chord in Western businessmen. It is interesting to note that of the "five fundamental factors" of strategy, Sun Tzu wrote that "the first (most important) of these factors is moral influence." The Chinese emphasis on the persuasion of general principles contrasts sharply with the Western notion of focusing on details and hammering out specifics in the narrow context of a legal framework.

When the U.S. and China negotiation teams hit a final stalemate after more than fifteen years of negotiating China's entry into WTO, Premier Zhu Rongji himself showed up at the negotiation table, shocking all present. USTR Charlene Barshevski was sticking tightly to the very fine legal language and nuances of the documents. Zhu simply waved his hand. The whole thing in his mind came down to several key issues, which he settled with vaguely drafted agreements and commitments to resolve the differences between both sides some time in the future—classic Chinese negotiation style. The Americans were not used to this, but the text was finished with a promise that both sides would fill in the details later. Over lunch, a cover page which would become the historic "China-US Bilateral Agreement Concerning Issues Relating to China's Entry into WTO" was drafted.

Solving Disputes

"There are some roads not to follow . . .
and some ground which should not be contested."

—SUN TZU

Chinese culture places a premium on harmony. Open conflict is something to be avoided. When disputes arise in a contract, the Chinese prefer to resolve them through amicable, non-binding conciliation talks between the parties. While amicable dispute settlement will probably be frustrating, time-consuming and not entirely amicable, it is still the preferred means. In fact, most Chinese contracts contain a provision emphasizing friendly negotiations in the event of disputes arising between the parties.

The Foreign Economic Contract Law stipulates in Article 37 that in the case of a dispute, contracting parties will do everything possible to settle it through consultation or mediation by a third party.

If the parties do not want to settle their dispute through consultation or third-party mediation, or if the consultation or mediation fails, they may submit the case to Chinese or other arbitration bodies according to the contract terms or a written agreement reached on arbitration after the dispute.

An example of a dispute being settled without a fight involved one US multinational first negotiating with the Chinese partner, a shareholding company; then going to the shareholders themselves to exert pressure; then turning to the Ministry of Light Industry, the administrative organ above the company; then going to what was then the State Council Production Office. As Sun Tzu's son Sun Ping once advised General Tian Chi, "To unravel a knot, you must not hold it tight. To settle a quarrel, you must not join in the fighting. If we leave what is knotted and attack what is loose, making further entanglement impossible, matters can be sorted out."

Many contracts contain an arbitration clause designating arbitration in third countries in the event that friendly negotiations become less than friendly. The objective from the Chinese side is to avoid open confrontation, and (short of arbitration) keep the relationship going.

The Final Stages

*"Nothing is more difficult than the art of manoeuvre.
What is difficult about manoeuvre is trying to make the most devious
route direct, and to turn misfortune into advantage."*

—SUN TZU

It is quite common for the Chinese to try to force reductions in the contract price in the last stages of discussion. Indeed, they will wait until the final touches are being put to negotiations—or at least appear to be. That is when they set the stage for driving an even harder bargain.

The Chinese know that once rumors of a concluded negotiation become public, the foreign firm will not be able to back down from the deal. To renege on a publicized China deal would mean embarrassment and necessary explanations to both stockholders and corporate headquarters. In one case, the contract was signed with a closing banquet and all the accompanying fanfare. When the contract was sent for approval, the higher authorities refused to approve it. The terms were apparently not to their liking. For the foreign firm, their reputation was on the line. The closing banquet had already been held, the photographs had been taken, and the news had spread back home. For the foreign firm, there was no pulling out.

One reason why the Chinese are not in a rush to make deals, according to some experts, is that they need to show their superiors what shrewd bargainers they are. "It won't make them feel good if you conclude the deal in the shortest time," said one China trader. "Go to see the Great Wall with them before beginning tough negotiations." Another tactic is to pepper your draft contract with a lot of points which unnecessarily and excessively favor the foreign side. The Chinese negotiators can then cut these out through the course of tough negotiations, and then report back to their superiors that substantial gains have been made at the negotiation table with the foreign side.

Once negotiations are over and everyone is getting ready to sign the contracts, foreign businessmen should try not to look too happy. The danger in doing so is that they might give the Chinese reason to suspect that they have been outdone in the agreement. As Sun Tzu wrote, "When capable, feign incapacity; when active, inactivity." In other words, smile but don't laugh.

PART II

Preparations for Negotiations

*"Master, according to the ancient arts,
how should one prepare for prolonged conflicts
and struggles?"*

*"Grasshopper, concentration on one's navel brings
inner power. Meditation is the answer."*

*"But Master, what if one's various
scheduling commitments do not allow enough
time for meditation?"*

*Sun Tzu advocated making advance preparations
as the basis of strategic planning before entering into a conflict
situation. This principle has become a basis of strategic planning for multinationals entering the China market. In
heeding Sun Tzu's advice, some multinationals will not
spare any expense in making adequate preparations.*

*When preparing for China negotiations, whether
at the due diligence, strategic planning, or boardroom decision-
making stages, most multinationals engage a host of various
professional advisers to help them with their difficulties and
to work through their frustrations.*

*At the same time, many multinationals find it
useful for their CEO to visit Beijing and correctly set the tone
of corporate policy to those high-ranking Chinese officials who
can influence the outcome of events. Visits such as these can
have a variety of repercussions for those on the ground who
later have to implement negotiations.*

Finding a Consultant

Shopping for Your Consultant

"What we need is a China consultant to help us with our joint venture," screamed the CEO as he banged his fist down on the conference table in frustration at the inability of his team of expatriate MBA specialists sent from corporate headquarters to effect the slightest headway in their China negotiations.

"Yes", replied the Asia-Pacific–Australia–Siberia Regional General Manager. "What we really need to find is a 'China expert.'"

There are a plethora of consultants today who regard themselves as "China experts." Many have been to China. Many have lived in China. Some even speak Mandarin.

The question is—what makes one person expert enough about China to be called a "China expert?"

"China expert?" quibbled one young banker working in a foreign bank's Beijing office. "How can anybody claim to be a 'China expert'? I was born and raised here. But the situation is changing all the time. It is impossible for anybody, even a Chinese, to keep up with what's happening. Even the different government departments don't know what the others are doing!"

"The problem with our company," explained the director of

a German company's legal department, "is that everybody who goes to China from our headquarters for a weeks trip, returns to Germany as a 'China expert'." Asking the consultant who he was seeking consultation from in Beijing, "As someone who has lived and worked in China for so many years, I mean as a real 'China expert', how do you feel about such situation when they arise?"

"I am sorry," replied the so-called 'China expert.' "After all these years in China, I am beginning to realize how little I actually know!"

The whole term "China expert"—like "Sinofile"—rings with a sort of colonial or imperialist peculiarity. Somehow Westerners feel that "experts" are needed to "understand the Chinese."

As one person who ventured into China with an idea that others said could not be done, later explained, "All the old China bores living in Hong Kong told me 'you have to live in China millions of years and speak Mandarin perfectly before you are able to deal with the Chinese.' I found out, however, that to deal with the Chinese is very easy. There is no secret. All you have to do is treat them like other people and they will be very receptive to what you want to do."

Putting the cloth shoe on the other foot, one Chinese scholar was sent to the East–West Centre in Hawaii for a graduate degree in American Studies. When asked by an American student what he was studying, the Chinese scholar replied, "American Studies."

"What's 'American Studies'?" asked the dumbfounded American student. "Research on per capita consumption of hot dogs and 'Big Macs'?"

"No," the Chinese graduate student replied gleefully, " 'American Studies' means that I study you."

When asked what qualified him as a China consultant, one consultant with a major Boston firm on his first business trip to China explained, "Our consulting firm is one of the biggest in Boston. We have done a lot of consulting for developing markets, in Latin American, for instance. Therefore, we are very experienced with developing markets. We have all the right theories and models."

Pricing Your Consultant

There are different kinds of China consultants. All are available for a price. The question is—what price, and what you will get for that price.

Many of these China consultants can be seen sitting around the lounge in the China World Hotel in Beijing, looking for bewildered multinational representatives (who are prime prey) as clients. Others appear regularly at seminars held in the China World Hotel where they expound graphically on the ins and outs of doing business in China to mesmerized audiences who spend more than US$500 to attend such seminars.

It is said that Robert Kwok, who built the China World Hotel and an empire of other five-star palaces in every major city in China, never consulted a China consultant.

Nevertheless, many multinationals feel that they must have a consultant by their side for a China deal, and are willing to pay the price. "We need them," explained one manager for the China region of a major US multinational. "Who else can we blame when the deal eventually goes wrong?"

Therefore, no regional manager will dare set foot upon an airplane to China without first consulting his China consultant—regardless of the price.

"Our China consultant demanded an 'unlimited expense account' before setting foot in China," complained one China manager. "We asked him why. He only answered, 'Well you know ... China is different.'"

One consulting firm in Hong Kong provides prospective multinational clients with three sets of price ranges. "We will close the deal for you," explained one partner of the firm with a puff on his cigar. "If you buy from us the highest-priced man hours, we will close the deal for you in three months. We call this high-priced man hour package 'active participation.' If you buy the second highest priced man hours, we will close it for you in six months. We call this middle-priced man hour package 'semi-active participation.' If you buy our lowest-priced man hour package, well ... it will take you a year to have the deal closed. That's because our involvement would be only through 'passive participation.'"

The prostitute slunk between the sofas in the lounge of a Shenzhen four-star hotel. She was wearing a skin-tight mini-skirt, her fingernails were painted a dainty pink, and her long hair was blown so that it hung everywhere. The tips of her hair were dyed pink to match her fingernails. As she tottered across the lobby on her inordinately high heels, the China manager of a major multinational thought about the consulting firm in Hong Kong and turned to his colleague asking, "Do you think she charges on the basis of 'active participation' or 'semi-active participation'?"

"I think, 'hyper-active participation,'" replied the colleague.

"Then what do you think is 'passive participation'?"

"It must mean they give you a corpse."

Bringing along Your Lawyer

Asset or Liability

The first thing not to do when negotiating in China is to bring your lawyer along. "You only bring your lawyer to the table when you really don't want to do the deal with the Chinese partner and need a polite excuse to allow the relationship to fall apart," explained one old 'China hand.' "When the whole thing breaks apart, you can always blame it on the lawyer and back out gracefully with a smile. You see, the trick is to use them for what they are good for—making problems. Otherwise it is simply not worth paying their fees!"

Some lawyers think otherwise, however. "Clients need us at the negotiation table," explained one 'Ivy League' American lawyer working in the Beijing office of a Wall Street firm. "We know the laws of China better than the Chinese and are not afraid to tell them so!"

As the legal counsel of one major American multinational famous for photo-imaging products explained, "I don't like 'China-type' lawyers who have lots of contacts in China. They value their contacts too much. We need lawyers who are advocates for our cause, and who are willing to stand up against the Chinese!" This legal counsel has been using one American law firm which advocates arbitration or advocates taking everything to court. This particular company has lots of experience negotiating in China because they have had to do a lot of it since.

One American lawyer stationed in the Beijing office of a major international law firm (with offices in every city of the world—the firm is often poetically referred to in the same breath as a major American fast food chain famous for selling greasy meat), was well known among the local Chinese lawyers because whenever he telephoned to discuss a dispute case he would go into a monologue criticizing China's legal system. "What kind of lawyers do you think you are? What kind of legal system do you think you have? What kind of legal system is this anyway? You don't have a real legal system here. Do you know that?"

When hiring lawyers to represent your company in China, one can see the obvious considerations of hiring one which has a far-reaching reputation, and has through all of his Ivy League training in "oriental law," developed a sensitive knowledge of the Chinese legal system.

One medium-sized listed European company visited one such British law firm in Shanghai only to be told by the senior partner there that as he has lived in Shanghai many years, he knew "everything" about Shanghai, and they should therefore be "privileged" to meet him. He shook their hands but added that he was "very busy" with "very big clients," warning them further that they would have to pay the bill for meeting him.

As one businessman commented about their billing rates: "Yes, I know them, aren't they a very famous firm of criminal lawyers?"

The Noble Profession

In the tradition of China's long history, lawyers were seldom used. Problems in China have always been settled through *guanxi*—"relations," and rarely through court. In fact, the old name for lawyers in China was song gun which translates into something like "litigation trickster," but connotates somebody who is really low class and a real "greaseball."

The term *gun* as used to describe lawyers in China, is defined in the Chinese–English dictionary published by the foreign languages publishing house, as a "scoundrel, rascal, or ruffian." The specific term for lawyer, *song gun* is defined in the same dictionary as a "legal pettifogger; shyster."

Therefore, when bringing your Wall Street or Central Hong Kong lawyer decked out in his gold cufflinks, gold collar pin, and suspenders to the negotiation table in China, you should be careful to find the appropriate Chinese expression when introducing him.

In America and England, a lawyer is treated with great respect. He is considered to be a "man of cloth," somebody who has received a higher education, somebody endowed with higher learning and greater knowledge. Lawyers convene their business proceedings in mahogany-paneled offices which have décor similar to funeral homes, giving them an aura of great seriousness. Therefore, when somebody in America or England says, "I am a lawyer," they usually say it with great pride, and expect to command the respect and obeisance of all those around them.

In China, the people are very practical. They respect businessmen who have money and assets. They respect you if you own a factory, a hotel, an office building; that is, if you have tangible assets to your name. On this basis, they can gauge whether you have really worked for a living and built up a real business or not. They view lawyers as people who do not have assets of their own (which are built up through hard work), but as cheap middlemen, who try to stick their noses into other people's business, who stay in between deals, thereby frustrating other people from making money, while charging a fee based on their time for wasting other people's time. If somebody says "I am a lawyer" in China, then they might as well be saying, "I am a used car dealer," "I am a middleman," or "I am a pimp."

In selecting the right law firm to accompany you through your very long China negotiations—and believe it, if you hire an expensive international law firm those negotiations are not going be short—one must know how to find out which law firms are soliciting clients eager to draw upon their knowledge and skills.

Choosing Counsel

A blind date with a lawyer can easily be accomplished by attending an American Chamber of Commerce luncheon held at a major hotel in China or Hong Kong. You will spot the lawyers immediately. Everyone else will be discussing real business. The lawyers will be the ones running around giving out their name cards to everyone in sight. One American lawyer in Hong Kong (also working for the greasy meat) would walk around each circular table handing out his name card to everyone seated before sitting down himself. After sitting down, he would try to demonstrate his Mandarin skills to everyone at the table by trying to get other Americans to speak with him in Mandarin.

When selecting a lawyer in Hong Kong for China negotiations, one must bear in mind that under the antiquated British legal system, which in Hong Kong is a historic leftover from the colonialist policies of the United Kingdom, one must select either a solicitor or a barrister, and not both. A solicitor sits in the office and charges his clients for his time. A barrister goes to court. A solicitor cannot do what a barrister does and a barrister cannot do what a solicitor does. Under the rules of the British system, a client cannot speak directly with a barrister (even if as human beings they both happen to speak the same language), but must hire a solicitor to listen to what the client has to say and speak of it to the barrister for the client. From this narrow aspect of this very narrow system, one can understand why the Chinese wanted to get rid of the British colonial system in its entirety in 1997.

In China, they have solicitors too. You can see them waiting for clients in the hotel lobbies in Shenzhen. Like their Hong Kong-British counterparts, they also charge by the hour for services rendered.

Losing Your Accountant

Consolidating Accounts

The "whiz-kid" sat diligently by his computer in his Hilton Hotel suite in Shanghai, picking at it. The joint venture which he was supposed to be acting as financial controller was far away in another province.

"Look," he exclaimed, impressed with his own discovery as the graph printouts begin to rattle out of his printer. "If we make soap bars, the joint venture is in the red. If we make detergent, it becomes profitable. If we double the volume, then it is really profitable. If we make automobiles, it is even more profitable. If we make airplanes, we will be rich...."

Accountants are an essential aspect of your China joint venture. You must bring one along to investigate your Chinese partner, carry out due diligence, and help you make critical decisions.

"The first thing we need as part of this due diligence," explained an accountant from one of the "big nine" accounting firms, "is all of an accounts of the Chinese partner." The accountant leaned across the table and implored the factory manager on the other side, "Can you give us your audited accounts?"

"Sure. Which set do you want?" replied the factory manager jovially.

"What do you mean 'which set'?" the international accountant piped up.

"We have many sets," explained the factory manager. "Which set do you want?"

"We want the fair, correct and true set, of course," the international accountant fired back.

"But they are all correct," explained the factory manager with a smirk.

"How can they all be correct when they are all different?" retorted the accountant.

"Oh, that's easy to explain", sighed the factory manager. "It just matters who you want to give them to. We have one set for the superior government organization we report to, one set for the tax authorities, one set for the Securities Commission for our planned Shanghai listing, one set for the public record, one set for our own internal profit distribution, one set to show to our own employees, and one set for foreign investors to look at. We assume you want the last set. Right?"

Fortunately for foreign investors, the "big nine" accounting firms are all in China. You can seek them out and speak to their management executives who will stare at you like frogs through their spectacles (which are usually as thick as the bottom of Coca Cola bottles). You can ask them questions. They will smile back. Because when they see you asking questions through the bottom of Coca Cola bottles, they will think you are a goldfish.

The Tax Man Cometh

China's tax system may seem like a labyrinth for the uninitiated. Fortunately, with the big accounting firms in China, you can find your way through the labyrinth and be assured that there are tax consultants who will make sure that you pay all the taxes which are necessary under China's laws. But before you pay all the taxes which the tax consultant will advise you to pay, you must first pay the tax consultant.

One foreign company had a tax problem and hired one of the big accounting firms to negotiate with the tax authorities. The tax consultant at the hired firm was a Taiwanese-American. The tax consultant however, never went to the tax authorities to negotiate the matter directly. Rather, he sent a local Chinese assistant.

The manager of the foreign company could not understand why there were so many problems with the tax authorities, and why they wanted these papers and those papers, then more and more papers on top of all the other papers. So the foreign manager telephoned the Taiwanese-American tax consultant at the big accounting firm and asked, "Why aren't you negotiating with these authorities instead of telling me to turn over whatever papers they want?"

"Oh, that is because we must do this as good professional tax consultants," replied the tax consultant.

"But I never handle my own negotiations in China like this," responded the foreigner.

"Well, we know how to handle the negotiations with the tax authorities, because we are professional tax consultants."

"Let me ask. Are you actually negotiating with them yourself?"

"Oh, no. Of course not. I am a professional tax consultant. My Chinese assistant is doing the negotiation."

"Let me speak with your assistant."

"What do you want me to do?" asked the assistant.

"I want you to negotiate with the tax authorities as that is what we are paying your big accounting firm to do for us and because your firm is so big and famous, we expect that you have some experience in this kind of matter or have done it before."

"Oh, we never do this kind of thing. I usually just ask on behalf of my boss what documents the tax authorities want. Then I go back to my boss and tell my boss what documents the tax authorities want. Then I go back to the tax authorities with the documents. Then I hear from the tax authorities what other documents they want. Then I go back to my boss to tell him. And then we get those documents and I go back to the tax authorities and submit them. And then when they want our client to pay, we tell the client how much they want our client to pay. Then we take instructions from the client. Then when the client does not want to pay, we then go back and ask the tax authorities whether or not they like the instructions ... then we ...."

The foreign manager slammed the phone down, rattling everything on his desk. He then had his driver take him and one Chinese assistant to the tax office.

"It is cheaper to just pay us what we want you to pay and then we'll forget about the rest," implored the local tax official. "You keep sending those big firm accountants here, they will cost you so much money. We know that they charge by the hour just to sit in traffic on their way to and from the office. This traffic time must cost you a lot of money. We don't want you to spend so much money in China. Just pay us directly and we will make things more simple. Forget about them!"

Nine months later, the foreign manager received a telephone call from the Taiwanese-American tax consultant at the big international accounting firm. "Ah, long time since we spoke. I am just calling to tell you that we have not heard anything from you for these past nine months and therefore thought it must be the appropriate time for us to send you a bill."

"A bill???"

"Yes, for the work we did last year."

"But we closed our annual books six months ago."

"Yes, but we spent so much time meeting with the tax authorities on your behalf last year. We are now just getting around to sending out the bill."

"But you only messed up everything, which I had to straighten out myself."

"You straightened everything out?"

"Yes, it was actually a very simple matter."

"You must have used corruption. We are a big international accounting firm and do everything right. Therefore there is no reason why you should settle this yourself. You should have used us and we would do it all by the book and this would be better for you. You see, in China there is the legal way and the illegal way and we always use the...."

"Stop right there. We used the legal way. We simply met with the tax authorities and found that there was no problem and you would have found the same if you had only gone there yourself."

"Then does that mean that I can send you the bill?"

"Of course not."

"But we spent many hours handling your case...."

Enter the CEO

Little Big Man

The Chinese often find how corporate executives in American companies pay so much deference to their CEOs perplexing. This is because the two systems differ greatly. In China, the government tells the State-owned enterprises what to do and the local CEOs must listen. This is because the money to support the State-owned enterprises comes from the government. In America, however, the CEOs tell the politicians what to do and they must listen because they cannot get re-elected unless the corporations agree to push the money for their election campaigns.

When one large American insurance company held a celebration in a Beijing hotel in honor of the second anniversary of the opening of its Beijing Resident Representative Office, its CEO attended. When this author offered to present a copy of one of his other books to the CEO, he was taken aside by the Beijing Chief Resident Representative and told condescendingly, "Maybe when you enter the room in which our dinner banquet in honor of our CEO is being held, you will have the opportunity to shake his hand. At that time, you may give him the book. But don't say anything else to him. His time is very precious. Our CEO is a very important and busy man, you know!"

American multinationals do not seem to realize that in China, their CEO is nothing! The leaders in the government can say "yes" or "no" to the investment plans of any multinational. So who then is the CEO? Chinese leaders smile tolerantly in photo sessions with CEOs who want to run back home after a 2-day pampered 5-Star China trip and pronounce, "I have opened the China market for our company." Little does the CEO realize how unimportant he is in the total scheme of everything in China.

When the CEO of one major American Oil Company came, he stayed in the most prestigious and luxurious hotel in Beijing. The staff of this American Oil Company's Beijing office, however, were on tenterhooks. They feared that something—anything—might go wrong. So they inspected every hotel room booked for CEO and his delegation of very high-powered executives.

Sure enough—something was not up to standard. The staff found that the hair dryers in the hotel were just not hot enough. The requisite head level for the CEOs hair dryer was that "it must have the speed and power to be able to proficiently dry the hair of their CEO within two minutes." Panic ensued. The staff went to the best department store in Beijing and bought a dozen of the most expensive imported hair dryers, putting one in each room for the CEO and members of his delegation.

Before the delegation arrived, one of the Senior Vice Presidents made no fewer than four trips to China to inspect every step of the way in which the company's CEO would walk. Finally, he found a trip-up. "At the Summer Palace, when the CEO and other members of our Board of Directors finish the boat trip, if it is late afternoon, or even dusk, it might be too dark and maybe someone may trip and fall into the water. We need to get torch lights!"

So the staff of the Beijing Representative Office went out and bought high-powered torch lights. These, however, were not suitable enough for the requisite climatic atmosphere to end the CEO's boat trip at the Summer Palace. So, Chinese girls were hired to wear Qing-dynasty style costumes and carry Chinese lanterns.

Despite the Senior Vice President's many trips to ensure that all was scheduled precisely, he had absent-mindedly allowed only two hours for the important Board of Directors' meeting being held that year in Beijing, because he was busily scheduling trips to different tourist sites and restaurants. Of course, the Board of Directors' meeting ran over two hours. The late morning meeting had to be cancelled; then lunch had to be cancelled. Then the meeting after lunch had to be cancelled. "Quick," panicked the CEO's assistant, "he will leave the meeting and go to the letter of intent signing without any lunch!" Turning to one of their Chinese staff, he ordered, "Quick, you must go to get him a sandwich. But it must be an 'American sandwich.' No other kind will do ... you know, pickles, and there must be some chips on the side." The poor girl ran across town in a taxi to one of the five-star hotels where such sandwiches could be created. The staff were exhausted by all the fuss. But the CEO was able to get to the letter of intent signing on time. He was even able to sit in the long hotel limousine on the way, and eat his sandwich alone. "We had nothing to eat all day," sighed the girl with exhaustion. "Finally, we Chinese staff and our Chief Representative sat down to some instant noodles. But our CEO was able to have his American sandwich!"

The CEO was afraid that when he arrived in China he

would not be able to make a telephone call from the point at which the plane touched down to the point at which he passed through Customs. The Beijing Office had to rent a special mobile phone at US$200 per day and have it couriered two weeks in advance of the CEO's arrival to the US, so he could carry the mobile phone with him and have it available in case he wanted to make a telephone call during the 15–20 minute period between airplane touchdown and Customs clearance.

The CEO arrived on the company's private plane. During the meeting, his wife did so much shopping in China that when it was time to leave, the private plane was overweight and could not take off. The CEO turned to the Asia-Pacific Regional President and said, "You can take another plane— maybe United Airlines...," leaving the Asia-Pacific Regional President behind.

Great Expectations

"Our CEO is coming to China next week and he wants to meet with Jiang Zemin!" said the Chief China Representative of an American multinational.

"I am sorry, but it is very difficult to arrange this at such short notice," explained the Chinese government official concerned.

"It doesn't matter. We must have a meeting with Jiang Zemin. Don't you know that the CEO of our company is a very important man?"

"But really, Jiang Zemin is the General Secretary of the world's largest Communist Party, and the head of State of the most populated country in the world."

"It does not matter. We are a big American multinational, and my CEO is a very important person. He can meet anybody he wants."

"But that is only if Jiang Zemin wants to meet him. And it isn't even Jiang's decision. It will have to go up through ministerial approval channels and then up to the State Council, and then over to Jiang's office. When did you say your CEO was coming?"

"Next week."

"Next week?"

"Yes. Next week."

"Then, this is impossible. Nobody can arrange a meeting with...."

"I insist. I must have this meeting arranged for my CEO. This is his first trip to China. He must have a meeting with Jiang Zemin."

"But who is your sponsor organization in China? I mean, who do you have existing joint ventures with?"

"We don't have any."

"What? Why not?"

"This is only exploratory."

"And you want your CEO to meet Jiang Zemin?"

"My CEO is an important man and knows many congressmen. He wants to tell Jiang Zemin to open up the China market to our company."

"That is impossible!"

"I insist that my CEO meet with Jiang Zemin."

"Well, we will have to see if there is any possible chance."

"My CEO is arriving next Tuesday night and leaving on Wednesday night."

"You mean he is only here for 24 hours?"

"Yes. So I think he will be available to meet Jiang Zemin for maybe a breakfast meeting at the hotel. I think 30 minutes is all they need. Otherwise, they will have to do it at lunch time."

"What about the rest of the time?"

"Oh, my CEO will have a very tight schedule."

"But this cannot be done. It is too tight. Notice is too short."

"Then, what do we do? My CEO has faxed us telling us to arrange a meeting with Jiang Zemin. We cannot tell him that this has not been done."

"All I can suggest is that you organize a meeting with someone else."

"OK. Li Peng."

"That is just as difficult as Jiang Zemin."

"OK. Zhu Rongji."

"That is just as difficult as Li Peng."

"Do you know this is exactly what my CEO wants to meet about? He wants to tell you guys to cut all this bureaucracy in China and open up the market. He cannot even see who he wants when he wants. This is not fair trade practice."

"But I just don't see how we can arrange a meeting for your CEO within the schedule he has given us at such short notice."

"OK. He has to see somebody. You tell me. What can be arranged?"

"Maybe the Second Vice Minister of the Ministry of Coal."

"Alright. I've had it with you guys. I am going to make a complaint to the American Embassy."

PART III

Sun Tzu's Art of War

*"Master, how does one perfect
the 'art of strategy'?"*

*"Grasshopper, the 'art of strategy'
is the 'artless art.'"*

*"But Master, what makes
the 'artless art' 'artless'?"*

*"Grasshopper, the artlessness of the
'artless art' is in the timelessness of the art and of
the artlessness in perfecting the art."*

*"Master, does that mean in perfecting
the art one can charge clients on the basis of
timeless billable hours?"*

CHAPTER 1

Strategic Assessments

Sun Tzu's *Art of War* can be applied to war, business, diplomacy, romance, office politics, and office romance. Obviously, it can be suitably applied to the preparing and handling of negotiations in China too. When making preparations for one's next round of joint venture or trade negotiations, it is advisable to consult the wisdom of "Master" Sun.

Sun Tzu said: War is a matter of vital importance to the State; a matter of life and death, the road either to survival or to ruin. Hence, it is imperative that it be thoroughly studied.

Therefore, to make assessment of the outcome of a war, one must compare the various conditions of the antagonistic sides in terms of the five constant factors: the first is moral influence; the second weather; the third, terrain; the fourth, commander; and the fifth, doctrine.

The Chinese always like to begin cooperation by establishing moral parameters. This is usually done by signing a letter of intent. Sometimes, at the letter of intent stage, the two sides are still very divergent in their ideas, or they do not have enough information about the other side to establish adequate commercial parameters. Nevertheless, the letter of intent must be signed to get the ball rolling.

The letter of intent is not legally binding. It is, however, "morally" binding. It is a set of principles which represents what the parties should believe about each other and what they believe the other has committed to. In effect, it is a statement of commitments which cannot necessarily be adhered to.

The trick in the letter of intent is to say as little as possible which is specific, while stating as much as possible which is moralistic. One must be prepared at the later contractual negotiations that the Chinese partner will recall the language of the letter of intent specifically, and remind the foreign partner that they are not living up to their moral agreement as stated in the letter of intent.

Moral influence means the way of inducing the people to be in complete accord with their sovereign, so that they will follow him regardless of their lives and without the slightest disloyalty. Weather signifies night and day, cold and heat, times and seasons. Terrain comprises distances, great and small; places, dangerous and secure; lands, open and constricted; and the chances of life and death. The commander stands for the general's qualities of wisdom, sincerity, benevolence, courage, and strictness. Doctrine refers to the principles guiding the organization of the army, the assignment of appropriate ranks to officers, and the control of military expenditure. These five constant factors should be familiar to every general. He who masters them wins, he who does not is defeated.

One foreign company signed a set of minutes with the Chinese party following their first real negotiation at the Jinbi Hotel in Shenzhen. The "Jinbi Minutes" were recalled over and over again during the course of three years of negotiations by the leader of the Chinese negotiation team. Finally, the head of the foreign negotiation team, who was on the verge of a nervous breakdown, screamed, "Damn it! Those Jinbi Minutes were signed three years ago and we didn't even know what the situation was then. Over these three years, this deal has changed. Over these three years, the capital required has changed. Over these three years, the technology has changed. Over these three years, the market in China has changed. So why can't you stop insisting on those Jinbi Minutes?"

Only then did the Chinese partner stop raising the Jinbi Minutes. Later, when the deal was finally done, contract signed, and business license issued, the leader of the Chinese party's negotiation team personally wrote the characters for "Jinbi Minutes" in calligraphy, had the calligraphy mounted on a Chinese scroll, and presented the scroll as a gift to the head of the foreign negotiation team, who by that time had already quit the company.

Therefore, to forecast the outcome of a war, the attributes of the antagonistic sides should be analysed by making the following seven comparisons:

(1) Which sovereign possesses greater moral influence?

Persuasiveness is the name of the game. The other side will tell you anything they think you want to hear and they will tell it to you in such a way that it will make you swallow it whole. You in turn will tell them all about your great technology and management skills even though your headquarters is riddled with politics and your boss cannot be reached because he is on a cruise. Think fast and talk smoothly. Do not believe what the other side is saying either.

(2) *Which commander is more capable?*

Just because the factory manager negotiating against you drinks Mao Tai and burps between gulps, do not think he does not know what he is up to. The darling MBAs on your negotiating team have probably never seen a factory in their lives. He has, and probably grown up in the one you are negotiating for. Do not underestimate him. He knows everything about the asset you think you are about to acquire.

(3) *Which side holds more favorable conditions in weather and terrain?*

The Chinese side will always know their own turf better than you do. Do not think that just because you speak Mandarin it means you know the terrain better—it only means you are more vulnerable because the Chinese team can communicate more garbage to you easier and at a faster rate. Do not think that you will be getting any benefit by hiring a Hong Kong or Taiwan Chinese either. They are about as faraway from the reality of the place as anyone else. They will stand in between you and the deal and, at the same time, most likely irritate or offend the other side.

(4) *On which side are decrees better implemented?*

Do not let your foreign lawyer influence your decisions with complaints like "China's laws aren't clear enough...." In fact, it is because of the lack of clarity that you can seek many commercial advantages. China is still a great place to make money because of the low level of regulation. Do not let the lawyers spoil this for you.

(5) Which side is superior in arms?

You may have the upper hand on this one. The Chinese are negotiating with you either for your technology or for cash, and it is probably the latter. After the negotiation, at the friendly farewell banquet, you will be expected to pay the bill.

(6) On which side are officers and men better trained?

"Better trained" in what? Your MBA darlings may be able to spread a host of beautiful statistics and graphics on the computer sheets but whether they can organize distribution and move products onto store shelves in China is something else.

(7) Which side is stricter and more impartial in meting out rewards and punishments?

The foreign executives will get their big fat bonuses and "hardship" packages whether the deal works or not. When something goes wrong on the Chinese side, the axe will fall on somebody.

By means of these seven elements, I can forecast victory or defeat.

If the sovereign heeds these stratagems of mine and acts upon them, he will surely win the war, and I shall, therefore, stay with him. If the sovereign neither heeds nor acts upon them, he will certainly suffer defeat, and I shall leave.

Having paid attention to the advantages of my stratagems, the commander must create a helpful situation over and beyond the ordinary rules. By "situation" I mean he should act expediently in accordance with what is advantageous in the field and so meet any exigency.

During the process of a long dispute settlement negotiation between a Chinese trading company and a major German multinational, the German representative, Director of the Chinese company, and the "dragon lady" named Madame Wang were in heated argument. In the middle of the argument, Madame Wang suddenly suggested to the German representative that after they resolve the dispute, she would like to apply for a position with the German company's China office. Imagine the reflection in the mind of the German representative upon hearing this proposal.

All warfare is based on deception. Therefore, when able to attack, we must pretend to be unable; when employing our forces, we must seem inactive; when we are near, we must make the enemy believe we are far away; when far away, we must make him believe we are near. Offer a bait to allure the enemy, when he covets small advantages; strike the enemy when he is in disorder. If he is well prepared with substantial strength, take double precautions against him. If he is powerful in action, evade him. If he is angry, seek to discourage him. If he appears humble, make him arrogant. If his forces have taken a good rest, wear them down. If his forces are united, divide them. Launch an attack where he is unprepared; take action when it is unexpected. These are the keys to victory for a strategist. However, it is impossible to formulate them in detail beforehand.

For the Western businessman, a negotiation in China may seem like a drawn, frustrating experience. This is because the Chinese will use every possible psychological and physiological ploy to wear down the opposite party. Mao Zedong advocated this policy. When fighting the Japanese and Kuomintang he urged the Red Army, "When the enemy is near, we run; when the enemy runs, we pursue; when the enemy is tired, we harass; when the enemy rests, we strike!"

Why should Western businessmen expect the veterans (or sons of veterans) of Mao's guerrilla victories to think any differently at the negotiation table than Mao? Even the great Chairman himself, admitted that his ideas came from Sun Tzu.

Through the concise and precise translation of Sun Tzu contained in this book, businessmen rushing off to China can gain easy and instant access to the mindset of Mao, and that of Mao's generation of protégé negotiators who will be greeting them at the airport on their arrival. Beware. Be prepared!

Now, the commander who gets many scores during the calculations in the temple before the war will have more likelihood of winning. The commander who gets few scores during the calculations in the temple before the war will have less chance of success. With many scores, one can win; with few scores, one cannot. How much less chance of victory has one who gets no scores at all? By examining the situation through these aspects, I can foresee who is likely to win or lose.

CHAPTER 2

Waging War

It is better to get one's China deal done efficiently, with the least waste of resources and expenditure of time. One does not want protracted negotiations, which can result in no results at all for the expenditure of money and personnel involved—and not to mention, the opportunity costs.

While an expedient negotiation may seem difficult to accomplish in an emerging and transitional market such as China, there are companies which succeed ... and, of course, there are those that do not. In some cases, a prolonged China negotiation is the fault of the Chinese ... in some cases however, it is not.

Sun Tzu said: Generally, operations of war involve one thousand swift chariots, one thousand heavy chariots and one hundred thousand mailed troops with the transportation of provisions for them over a thousand li. Thus the expenditure at home and in the field, the stipends for the entertainment of State guests and diplomatic envoys, the cost of materials such as glue and lacquer and the expense for care and maintenance of chariots and armor, will come to an immense amount of money each day. An army of one hundred thousand men can be raised only when sufficient financial resources are available.

Some multinationals are convinced that their financial resources can buy market entry into China. They therefore embark on elaborate plans. Strategic planning sessions drag on over the course of days, even weeks. These strategic planning executives fly into Hong Kong and Beijing from Tokyo, Detroit and New York to share all their views and exchange their many different opinions.

Hotels must be booked and limousines sent to the airports to collect all of the strategically thinking executives so as to comfortably transport them to the hotel. Large suites must be arranged so that they can have space in which to allow their deep-thinking strategic minds to strategize.

Conference rooms must be booked and meals must be planned. Decisive coffee breaks must be carefully timed. Evening social activities must be arranged so that the hard-working executives can rest their weary strategically thinking executive minds.

All of this must be charged back to the right corporate accounts so that there are no mistakes and none of the executives are inconvenienced by having to pay for something out of their own pockets. On top of this, every executive must have proper airline bookings reconfirmed so that whether the meetings are over or not, they can all fly back home to spend weekends with their families.

Compare this style to the conditions under which the Chinese counterpart negotiating team will operate.

In directing such an enormous army, a speedy victory is the main object. If the war is long delayed, the men's weapons will be blunted and their armor will be dampened. If the army attacks cities, their strength will be exhausted. Again, if the army engages in protracted campaigns, the resources of the State will not suffice. Now, when your weapons are blunted, your armor dampened, your strength exhausted and your treasure spent, neighboring rulers will take advantage of your distress to act. In this case, no man, however wise, is able to avert the disastrous consequences that ensue. Thus, while we have heard of stupid haste in war, we have not yet seen a clever operation that was prolonged. There has never been a case in which a prolonged war has benefited a country. Therefore, only those who understand the dangers inherent in employing troops know how to conduct war in the most profitable way.

One major American multinational sought to enter China's market. Despite the advice given to this multinational by many who had already set up successful operations in China (that is, it was best to go to the "grassroots" and tie up one joint venture partner after another), this multinational had grandiose plans. It wanted to tie up every one of China's factories in a single industrial sector in one big negotiation package with the central government.

This strategy was deemed to be the right approach as it was formulated during many of the types of strategic-planning sessions described above. How it came to be perceived by the senior management that the Chinese central government would actually even consider allowing an American multinational to tie up one of China's entire industries in a foreign-controlled monopoly can only be accredited to the combined brain power of all of these strategically thinking executives who had flown from all over the world to different places, to exchange valuable thoughts and opinions at very elaborately organized meetings.

Those adept in employing troops do not require a second levy of conscripts or more than two provisionings. They carry military supplies from the homeland and make up for their provisions by relying on the enemy. Thus the army will be always be plentifully provided.

Teams of American executives were assigned as members of the negotiating "task force" which was to be stationed in Beijing to carry out the long and arduous negotiation with the Chinese central government. As it turned out, none of the executives ever moved to Beijing because they all had families. They all had to move to Hong Kong to take up residences in homes that were equivalent to what they had left behind in America. After six to nine months of relocating all of these executives to Hong Kong, putting all of their children in the International American School, and arranging for all their wives to join social organizations to keep them busy, the executives began commuting to Beijing every week for negotiations. They would fly in on Monday or Tuesday, and fly back on Thursday or Friday.

When a country is impoverished by military operations, it is because an army far from its homeland needs a distant transportation. Being forced to carry supplies over great distances renders the people destitute. On the other hand, the local price of commodities normally rises in the area near the military camps. The rising prices cause financial resources to be drained away. When the resources are exhausted, the peasantry will be afflicted with urgent exactions. With this depletion of strength and exhaustion of wealth, every household in the homeland is left empty. Seven-tenths of the people's income is dissipated and six-tenths of the government's revenue is paid for broken-down chariots, worn-out horses, armor and helmets, arrows and crossbows, halberds and bucklers, spears and body shields, draught oxen and heavy wagons.

Meanwhile, their competition moved into the market, stationing executives in China in low-keyed positions, at much lower overheads than the "task force." The competition began to tie up Chinese partners one by one at the local level.

Hence, a wise general is sure of getting provisions from the enemy countries. One zhong of grains obtained from the local area is equal to twenty zhong shipped form the home country; one dan of fodder in the conquered area is equal to twenty dan from the domestic store.

The Chinese central government provided a counterpart negotiation team for the American multinational's negotiation team. However, the Chinese central government negotiation team could not control the local factories. So in this regard, the negotiation was somewhat pointless. Nevertheless, the American multinational thought that this was a good strategic approach and continued the negotiation for a very long time. Millions of dollars were spent supporting the entire operation.

Now in order to kill the enemy, our men must be roused to anger; to gain the enemy's property, our men must be rewarded with war trophies. Accordingly, in chariot battle, when more than ten chariots have been captured, those who took the enemy chariot first should be rewarded. Then, the enemy's flags and banners should be replaced with ours; the captured chariots mixed with ours and mounted by our men. The prisoners of war should be kindly treated and kept. This is called "becoming stronger in the course of defeating the enemy."

Finally the Chinese suggested, "OK, if you want to take over all of our factories in this particular industry, we might consider giving them to you ... provided that you first pay off all their outstanding cross and triangle debts and clear their outstanding receivables!"

Hence, what is valued in war is a quick victory, not prolonged operations. And therefore the general who understands war is the controller of his people's fate and the guarantor of the security of the nation.

Sure enough, this decision to pick up the triangle debts and outstanding receivables was worth it. This multinational corporation took over all but one of the factories within its particular consumer products sector, merged them together into a single corporate structure, in turn monopolizing the industry.

Today China accounts for the second largest sales market of products for this multinational next to the U.S. market. Growth potential in China could one day make it the largest. So while the Chinese government negotiation team appeared to be the winners passing their state-owned enterprise problems to the foreign investor, in the end, the foreign investor took the market, and today is industry kingpin.

To a great extent, it all comes down to a question of perceptions. In China business today, both government and enterprise tend to think short-term, often disregarding long-term strategic interests largely because they have so many immediate problems on their plate. The future in many China market segments will belong to foreign multi-nationals which have the vision to develop the industry as opposed to thinking about short term immediate personal interests (which is why corruption has eaten China's business and government structure to the roots).

In the future of Chinese business we may ask in the end, who read and understood Sun Tzu better?

CHAPTER 3

Attack by Stratagem

Sun Tzu taught that rash action will always lead to defeat. One must proceed upon a carefully thought-out plan. In China, direct argumentation at the negotiation table will only result in disaster. One should always think carefully before one speaks. Emotionalism must be eliminated from the negotiation stratagem.

> *Sun Tzu said: Generally, in war, the best thing of all is to take the enemy's state whole and intact, to ruin it is inferior to this. To capture the enemy's entire army is better than to destroy it; to take intact a battalion, a company or a five-man squad is better than to destroy them. Hence, to win one hundred victories in one hundred battles is not the acme of skill. To subdue the enemy without fighting is the supreme excellence.*

One European company was frustrated when their Chinese partner delayed submitting the joint venture documents for approval after agreement of all terms and conditions was complete, despite the Chairman of the Chinese party's many promises to do so. Finally, through investigations, their advisor in Beijing found out that the Chinese party was receiving a special State policy loan bearing low interest—allocated on the principle of assisting ailing State enterprises in keeping afloat in China's increasingly competitive market that is internationalized by foreign brand competition through joint ventures.

The Chinese party obviously wanted to delay the joint venture approval until after it had drawn down the entire amount of its loan from the State. If the State knew that the Chinese party would receive funds from a foreign investor, they would, of course, immediately cut the loan.

Thus, the best policy in war is to attack the enemy's strategy. The second best way is to disrupt his alliances through diplomatic means. The next best method is to attack his army in the field. The worst policy is to attack walled cities. Attacking cities is the last resort when there is no alternative. It takes at least three months to get mantelets and shielded vehicles ready and to prepare the necessary arms and equipment. It takes at least another three months to pile up earthen mounds against the walls. The general unable to control his impatience will order his troops to swarm up the wall like ants with the result that one third of them will be slain, while the cities remain untaken. Such is the calamity of attacking walled cities.

Most investors would have lost patience, walked away from the deal, or shown their temper to the Chinese, in turn losing the deal altogether. This investor, however, wanted the deal—intact.

Therefore, those skilled in war subdue the enemy's army without fighting. They capture the enemy's cities without assaulting them and overthrow his state without protracted operations. Their aim must be to take all under heaven intact through strategic superiority. Thus, their troops are not worn out and their triumph will be complete. This is the art of attacking by stratagem.

The investors therefore attacked the Chinese party's strategy by going to the different departments at the central government level responsible for approving and allocating the loan. By talking with these various departments, they disrupted the Chinese party's alliances. As soon as these departments realized that they were lending funds through a policy loan allocation which could otherwise be replaced by a direct foreign investment, they summoned the Chairman of the Chinese party to Beijing and informed him that his loan would be promptly cancelled.

Consequently, the art of using troops is this: When ten to the enemy's one, surround him. When five times his strength, attack him. If double his strength, divide him. If equally matched, be capable of engaging him. If less in number, be capable of withdrawing. And if in all respects unfavorable, be capable of eluding him. Hence, a weak force will eventually fall captive to a strong one if it simply holds ground and conducts a desperate defense.

Shortly thereafter, the Chairman of the Chinese party, who had formerly behaved in a heavy-handed manner, came with a delegation of his enterprise's managers to the representative office of the foreign company in Shanghai. His desperate defense was that they were now eager and willing to submit the documents as quickly as possible and to get on with the joint venture. Essentially, the foreign party had succeeded in attacking the Chairman's strategy.

Now, the general is the bulwark of the State: If the bulwark is com-

plete at all points, the State will surely be strong; if the bulwark is defective, the State will certainly be weak.

Unfortunately, a new leader had been placed at the head of the foreign party's negotiation team. She was a fat Italian woman who was herself a prima donna. She felt that what had been achieved was just not enough. She wanted to attack the Chinese party's Chairman as an individual. She wanted to exert her own influence.

Now, there are three ways in which a sovereign can bring misfortune upon his army:

(1) By ordering an advance while ignorant of the fact that the army cannot go forward, or by ordering a retreat while ignorant of the fact that the army cannot fall back. This is described as "hobbling the army."

The Italian woman leading the negotiation team decided to insist that the Chairman of the Chinese party could not be the Chairman of the future joint venture. She wanted to accuse him of "lying" in front of his own managers. She did not consider, despite the advice of others, the fact that this Chairman had been Chairman of the Chinese enterprise for over a decade, and she underestimated the loyalty of his subordinates.

(2) By interfering with the army's administration without knowledge of the internal affairs of the army. This causes officers and soldiers to be perplexed.

The Italian woman further interfered with the internal administration of the foreign company's Shanghai representative office. She did not listen to the reports and opinions of its senior person who was Director for Asia-Pacific operations, and who had been personally handling all aspects of the negotiation with the Chinese party. Instead, she listened to her accountant who was a squeamish MBA type, who kept piping what the fat lady wanted to hear: "We can't let him be Chairman of the joint venture. The lawyers say that the Chairman has legal authority to sign away all the assets. Anything could happen because he lied to us once and this is China you know.... We must tell him to his face that he cannot be Chairman, and make our intentions perfectly clear!"

Everybody else in the foreign company's Shanghai office tried to explain that in virtually every joint venture in China, the Chinese partner appoints the Chairman of the Board. Their explanations went unheard and ignored.

(3) By interfering with the direction of fighting, while ignorant of the military principle of adaptation to circumstances. This shows doubts and misgivings in the minds of his officers and soldiers.

When the Chairman of the Chinese enterprise showed up to meet with the Italian lady leading the foreign negotiation team, the woman immediately told the Chairman, "You cannot be the Chairman of the Board of the joint venture because you lied to us and we cannot accept liars."

The Chairman immediately lost face in front of his own managers. Cleverly, however, he said to her, "This is very confusing. I do not know whether you are speaking for yourself or for your company. However, I would like to receive your comments in writing from your company's Board of Directors and signed by the Board." He and his managers then left.

If the army is confused and suspicious, neighboring rulers will take advantage of this and cause trouble. This is simply bringing anarchy into the army and flinging victory away.

Thus, there are five points in which victory may be predicted:

(1) He who knows when to fight and when not to fight will win.
(2) He who understands how to handle both superior and inferior forces will win.
(3) He whose ranks are united in purpose will win.
(4) He who is well prepared and lies in wait for an enemy who is not well prepared will win.
(5) He whose generals are able and not interfered with by the sovereign will win.
It is in these five points that the way to victory is known.

As the Chinese party's Chairman and his managers left the room, a dim silence fell over the faces of all of the foreign party's staff who had been tirelessly negotiating the project on the ground in China for over two years. Only the sound of smoke spiraling pointlessly upwards from the cigarette held by the Italian lady between her thumb like forefingers could be heard.

"Did he say I had to give him our position in a letter from our company's Board of Directors?" the Italian lady asked in disbelief, knowing the repercussions from headquarters upon realizing that the hard-won deal had been lost in a last minute act of tactlessness. "Yes," replied the Director for Asia-Pacific. He asked for a letter from our Board."

Therefore, I say: Know the enemy and know yourself, and you can fight a hundred battles with no danger of defeat. When you are igno-

rant of the enemy but know yourself, your chances of winning and losing are equal. If ignorant both of your enemy and of yourself you are sure to be defeated in every battle.

The Director for Asia-Pacific was furious that the Italian lady had shattered nearly two years of negotiations in hammering out what could have been a final deal. He cleverly requested the team's lawyer to write a factual "witness report" and submitted this to the corporate legal counsel at headquarters for his opinion on what to do next.

In this particular German company, the corporate counsel also served on the supervisory board, a body within German corporate structures which has authority to supervise actions of individual directors on the board to protect shareholder interests. The report on the Italian lady director's rampaging negotiation was soon circulated to the other board members who had been looking forward to seeing the China deal go through. Of course, they were not prepared to issue any such letter supporting her position.

She was soon under scrutiny and eventually resigned, decrying the lawyer who wrote the witness report as adopting Cultural Revolution Red Guard tactics to do her in. She even cursed him saying he had "graduated from the Patty Hearst School of Law." When news of her resignation resounded back to China, both foreign and Chinese negotiators resumed discussions, this time over a bottle of Bollinger champagne in celebration.

CHAPTER 4

Disposition of Military Strength

In preparing for disputes, one must protect oneself from the outset. While good personal relations are critical in any China deal, one must remember that individuals may change and personalities can be volatile. It is very important to always prepare for the worst. One way of doing this is to use careful arbitration language in the China contract. Yet, does strongly worded language really help when the deal goes sour?

> *Sun Tzu said. The skilful warriors in ancient times first made themselves invincible and then awaited the enemy's moment of vulnerability. Invincibility depends on oneself, but the enemy's vulnerability on himself. It follows that those skilled in war can make themselves invincible but cannot cause an enemy to be certainly vulnerable. Therefore, it can be said that one may know how to achieve victory, but cannot necessarily do so.*

In the West, when one party breaks a contractual obligation, the other party will argue, yell and scream, and then sue them in court. This, in the minds of Chinese, is brutal and unnecessary behavior. Sun Tzu preached the art of defense as the precondition for offensive attack.

Invincibility lies in the defense, the possibility of victory in the attack. Defend yourself when the strength is inadequate, and attack the enemy when it is abundant. Those who are skilled in defense hide themselves as under the most secret recesses of earth; those skilled in attack flash forth as from above the topmost heights of heaven. Thus, they are capable both of protecting themselves and of gaining a complete victory.

The Chinese dispute resolution process is akin to both parties gradually sliding down a slippery slope. While they would like to be successfully cooperating at the top, they in fact see their relationship continue to disintegrate as they gropingly slide downwards. This contrasts with Western litigation, which in the Chinese mind, is akin to having one party push the other off a cliff.

To foresee a victory no better than ordinary people's foresight is not the acme of excellence. Neither is it the acme of excellence if you win a victory through fierce fighting and the whole empire says, "Well done!" Hence, by analogy, to lift an autumn hair does not signify great strength; to see the sun and moon does not signify good sight; to hear the thunderclap does not signify acute hearing. In ancient times, those called skilled in war conquered an enemy easily conquered.

In China, most contracts provide that the parties must resolve their dispute through negotiations or mediation before going to arbitration, thereby avoiding litigation altogether. A typical arbitration clause will read something like this:

"In the event of a dispute, both parties will seek to resolve their differences through friendly negotiations. In the event that they are unable to resolve their dispute through friendly negotiations, then either party may submit the dispute to arbitration at the China International Economic and Trade Arbitration Commission."

The question which one must ask from the point of legal language is, what actually qualifies as "friendly negotiations"? In the event that the negotiations are continually not friendly, then can this lack of friendliness prevent either party from having any legal right to submit the case to arbitration at all?

Consequently, a master of war wins victories without showing his brilliant military success, and without gaining the reputation for wisdom or the merit for valor. He wins his victories without making mistakes. Making no mistakes is what establishes the certainty already of victory, for it means that he conquers an enemy defeated. Accordingly, a wise commander always ensures that his forces are put in an invincible position, and at the same time will be sure to miss no opportunity to defeat the enemy. It follows that a triumphant army will not fight with the enemy until the victory is assured, while an army destined to defeat will always fight with his opponent first, in the hope that it may win by sheer good luck. The commander adept in war enhances the moral influence and adheres to the laws and regulations. Thus it is in his power to control success.

The term "friendly" is defined in the Chinese–English dictionary as "friend," "friendly," "profound friendship," "appropriate friend." Presumably, for instance, if the foreign party wished to carry out arbitration procedures rather than serve a writ as in the West, it would have to first express itself in any of the above terms at the negotiation table in advance of implementing pro-

cedures so as to meet the requisite legal standard of "friendliness" and qualify as being in an adequate state of rejection, so
as to submit the whole affair to arbitration.

The question to ask then is, if you want to back out of your
China deal, how "friendly" a disposition do you have to display
to the other party before your negotiations qualify as "friendly
negotiations?" Is it necessary to send flowers to the negotiating
table?

This question has now become of great interest to foreign
law firms advising clients on arbitration disputes. These law
firms have already begun to equip staff with the necessary
knowledge in preparation for providing "expert witnesses" to
give commentary to the China International Economic and
Trade Arbitration Commission as to whether or not the parties
have met the adequate threshold of friendliness. Imagine the
enormous billing opportunity which the legal question of ascer-
taining appropriate evidence of friendliness can provide to the
legal profession.

> Now, the elements of the art of war are first, the measurement of
> space; second, the estimation of quantities; third, calculations of fig-
> ures; fourth, comparisons of strength; and fifth, chances of victory.
> Measurements of space are derived from the ground. Quantities derive
> from measurement, figures from quantities, comparisons from figures
> and victory from comparisons. Therefore, a victorious army is as a
> hundredweight balanced against a grain, and a defeated army is as
> a grain balanced against a hundredweight.

While many Hong Kong law firms have built their fortunes
on partners supervising hundreds of clerks filling out forms
used for property transfers in the conveyancing industry,
American law firms with offices in China can now hire hun-

dreds of "expert witnesses" professing deep knowledge of the necessary expressions and behavior required in China to meet the legal threshold of adequate friendliness, in order to say that this criteria has been fulfilled to allow a dispute to move from "friendly negotiations" to arbitration.

A number of specialists have considered the extent to which one must express their "friendliness" in their negotiations. In some cases, friendliness needs to be expressed through inviting the party with which you have a dispute to a lengthy dinner and karaoke entertainment. Afterwards, some specialists consider that this in itself is not enough, and karaoke must be followed by massage and sauna treatment.

It is even rumored that some State organs are getting on the bandwagon as they had before, setting up consulting companies to cash in on the front load investment (for example, you must use the consulting company of the local Planning Commission to prepare your feasibility study if you want it to be approved by the Planning Commission). They are now considering setting up special "friendliness evaluation centers" to cash in on the "friendliness" issue relating to the back-end load of getting out of the deal through dispute resolution.

An army superior in strength takes action like the bursting of pent-up waters into a chasm of a thousand fathoms deep. This is what the disposition of military strength means in the actions of war.

CHAPTER 5

Use of Energy

Sun Tzu believed that the big force does not necessarily guarantee victory. Rather, victory lies in the concentration of forces regardless of their size and the efficiency in their employment.

In China, big negotiation teams do not always mean efficiency. Likewise, the expensive big name law firm or accountancy or management consultancy does not always mean effectiveness in China. If you need to run to your embassy in China to seek assistance, you can be assured that you are really in trouble.

Sun Tzu said: Generally, management of a large force is the same in principle as the management of a few men: It is a matter of organization. And to direct a large army to fight is the same as directing a small one. It is a matter of command signs and signals. That the whole army can sustain the enemy's all-out attack without suffering defeat is due to operations of extraordinary and normal forces. Troops thrown against the enemy as a grindstone against eggs is an example of the strong beating the weak.

When one large European pharmaceutical company had its

trademark infringed in China, they called upon one of the big Hong Kong law firms to help with the dispute. The British solicitor in the law firm wrote pages and pages of briefs and affidavits to submit to the China Trademark Office. The entire paper was so heavy that they would have been better off threatening to hit the trademark official with it rather than asking him to read it. The result was that nobody in the China Trademark Office would so much as bother reading this verbose text. It sat in the "in box" and nothing happened for weeks. This is an example of throwing eggs at a grindstone.

Generally, in battle, use the normal force to engage and use the extraordinary to win. Now, to a commander adept at the use of extraordinary forces, his resources are as infinite as the heaven and earth, as inexhaustible as the flow of the running rivers. They end and begin again like the motions of the sun and moon. They die away and then are reborn like the changing of the four seasons. There are not more than five musical notes, but the various combinations of the five notes bring about more melodies than can ever be heard. There are not more than five basic pigments, yet in blending them together it is possible to produce more colors than can ever be seen. There are not more than five cardinal tastes, but the mixture of the five yields more flavors than can ever be tasted.

The pharmaceutical company decided they had better diversify their tactics. While keeping their British solicitor on a retainer—he insisted that "the Chinese must reply to my letter ... otherwise it is not proper and ethical and we cannot move on to the next stage of dispute resolution"—they decided to engage some experienced China advisers who had a more practical approach.

In battle, there are not more than two kinds of postures—operation of the extraordinary force and operation of the normal force, but their combinations give rise to an endless series of manoeuvres. For these two forces are mutually reproductive. It is like moving in a circle, never coming to an end. Who can exhaust the possibilities of their combinations?

The China advisers suggested putting the foreign pharmaceutical company's request and related argument on a one-page document. "The Trademark Office officials won't bother reading any more," explained the outside adviser. He then took the one page and held a private meeting with the Trademark Office officials. He also had Chinese contacts within the Trademark Office lobby for the position. Only then did he organize a formal meeting between the foreign pharmaceutical company and the Director of the China Trademark Office.

When torrential water tosses boulders, it is because of its momentum; when the strike of a hawk breaks the body of its prey, it is because of timing. Thus, in battle, a good commander creates a posture releasing an irresistible and overwhelming momentum, and his attack is precisely timed in a quick tempo. The energy is similar to a fully drawn crossbow; the timing, the release of the trigger.

The Director of the Trademark Office complained that they had too many cases to solve. The Trademark Office was very busy. If a promise of positive statements and publicity from the foreign pharmaceutical company could be put on the table, if the Trademark Office came out with a favorable decision— well, maybe something could be arranged.

Amid turmoil and tumult of battle, there may be seeming disorder and yet no real disorder in one's own troops. In the midst of confusion and chaos, your troops appear to be milling about in circles, yet it is proof against defeat.

Meanwhile, an American Trade Representative and his negotiators were back for their annual intellectual property rights talks and threatening trade sanctions.

Apparent disorder is born of order; apparent cowardice, of courage; apparent weakness, of strength. Order or disorder depends on organization and direction; courage or cowardice on postures; strength or weakness on dispositions.

Fists were slamming tables and a lot of emotion was spurting in many different directions. America threatened sanctions. China threatened counter-sanctions. America had to back down. China had to deliver a result. Amidst all this excitement, the European pharmaceutical company remained calm and low-keyed, and more quiet lobbying was done at the top using subtle relations.

Thus, one who is adept at keeping the enemy on the move maintains deceitful appearances, according to which the enemy will act. He lures with something that the enemy is certain to take. By so doing he keeps the enemy on the move and then waits fore the right moment to make a sudden ambush with picked troops.

The European company quietly pressed its case. Praises of China's system for protecting intellectual property were put on the table before the results. Quiet persistence and subtle lobbying wnsued. Then there was the horse trade: "We'll hold a big press conference to announce how China has protected our intellectual property rights and tell the world about the wonderful protection provided under the laws of China if you guys settle this issue!" Then it came—a result. The Trademark Office put the European pharmaceutical company's case on the top of its long pile of American cases. Priority was given and a result decreed.

> *Therefore, a skilled commander sets great store by using the situation to the best advantage, and does not make excessive demands on his subordinates. Hence he is able to select the right men and exploit the situation. He who takes advantage of the situation uses his men in fighting as rolling logs or rocks. It is the nature of logs and rocks to stay stationary on the flat ground, and to roll forward on a slope. If four-cornered, they stop; if round-shaped, they roll. Thus, the energy of troops skillfully commanded is just like the momentum of round rocks quickly tumbling down from a mountain thousands of feet in height. This is what "use of energy" means.*

CHAPTER 6

Weaknesses and Strengths

As mentioned earlier, for Western businessmen, a negotiation in China may seem like grueling chinese torture. This is because the Chinese are aware that most Western businessmen are impatient. These businessmen come to China with a fixed time schedule. Their hotels and air tickets are booked in advance. Meetings are also arranged in advance down to the last minute. At least the executives think they are, that is, until they get off the airplanes. That is when they realize they have really arrived in China, and reality sets in.

Sun Tzu said: Generally, he who occupies the field of battle first and awaits his enemy is at ease; he who arrives later and joins battle in haste is weary. And, therefore, one skilled in war brings the enemy to the field of battle and is not brought there by him.

The Chinese like to dictate the pace of negotiations and the agenda. Little does the unwary Western businessman realize that the real negotiating begins at the moment of arrival in China. In fact, the first-time visitor will invariably feel off-guard.

One able to make the enemy come of his own accord does so by offer-
ing him some advantage. And one able to stop him from coming does
so by inflicting damage on him. Thus, when the enemy is at ease, he
is able to tire him; when well fed, to starve him; when at rest, to make
him move. Appear at points which the enemy must hasten to defend,
move swiftly to places where he is not expected.

On one visit, a Western businessman may find his Chinese
hosts waiting to greet him before going through Customs. On
another visit, the same businessman may have to wait outside in
a milling airport crowd until found by the representative of his
host organization. Regardless, even if visitors take preparatory
measures (for example, booking their own hotels in advance),
their Chinese hosts ultimately control the schedule.

That you may march a thousand li without tiring yourself is
because you travel where there is no enemy. That you are certain to
take what you attack is because you attack a place the enemy does
not or cannot protect. That you are certain of success in holding
what you defend is because you defend a place the enemy does not or
cannot attack.

Therefore, against those skilful in attack, the enemy does not
know where to defend, and against the experts in defense, the enemy
does not know where to attack.

Controlling the other party's schedule gives the Chinese the
advantage of an element of surprise. Beware the visitor who
arrives ready to hit the negotiating table. His hosts may have a
few sightseeing tours lined up (for example, a full-day's drive to
the Great Wall and back, followed by a heavy Peking Duck
dinner) for their jetlagged guest.

How subtle and insubstantial, that the expert leaves no trace. How divinely mysterious, that he is inaudible. Thus, he is master of his enemy's fate.

His offensive will be irresistible if he plunges into the enemy's weak points; he cannot be overtaken when he withdraws if he moves swiftly. Hence, if we wish to fight, the enemy will be compelled to an engagement even though he is safe behind high ramparts and deep ditches. This is because we attack a position he must relieve. If we do not wish to fight, we can prevent him from engaging us even though the lines of our encampment be merely traces out on the ground. This is because we divert him from going where he wishes.

This was what Richard H. Solomon, former Assistant Secretary of State to Henry Kissinger, realized when he stepped off the plane at Beijing's Capital Airport in 1975. He had come to negotiate a communiqué. Like most State Department officials, he arrived ready to "hit the ground running" and to negotiate the kind of communiqué that would be full of all the "right stuff." Right? Not so!

Accordingly, by exposing the enemy's dispositions and remaining invisible ourselves, we can keep our forces concentrated, while the enemy must be divided. We can form a single united body at one place, while the enemy must scatter his forces at ten places. Thus, it is ten to one when we attack him at one place, which means we are numerically superior. And if we are able to use many to strike few at the selected place, those we deal with will be in dire straits.

The first thing on Solomon's agenda was not a negotiation. "They invited us out to a picnic in the Western Hills," Solomon recalled in later years. "Kissinger was going crazy."

The spot where we intend to fight must not be made known. In this way, the enemy must take precautions at many places against the attack. The more places he must guard, the fewer his troops we shall have to face at any given point.

The Chinese kept the entire American State Department delegation hanging at the edge trying to figure out what was next on the agenda. The Americans spent the entire time chomping at the bit waiting for some real negotiation to begin.

For if he prepares to the front, his rear will be weak; and if to the rear, his front will be fragile. If he strengthens his left, his right will be vulnerable; and if his right gets strengthened, there will be few troops on his left. If he sends reinforcements everywhere, he will be weak everywhere. Numerical weakness comes from having to prepare against possible attacks; numerical strength from compelling the enemy to make these preparations against us.

"The Chinese were dragging things out," described Solomon. Hoping that the Americans would give in rather than miss their self-imposed deadline, the Chinese waited until the last minute. "Then, they gave him [Kissinger] an unacceptable document at midnight on the last day of the visit."

Therefore, if one knows the place and time of the coming battle, his troops can march a thousand li and fight on the field. But if one knows neither the spot nor the time, then one cannot manage to have the left wing help the right wing or the right help the left; the forces in the front will be unable to support the rear, and the rear will be unable to reinforce the front.

All too often Western businessmen come to China with big

talk and too much anxiety to sign a contract, without fully realizing what they are plunging into.

How much more so if the furthest portions of the troop deployments extend tens of li in breadth, and even the nearest troops are separated by several li!

The Chinese party always wants to conduct negotiations at its own factory, in its own territory, luring its foreign counterpart away from supply lines such as efficient business centers and clean bathrooms. Moreover, the Chinese party can control the negotiation schedule at their factory which is usually divided into long banquets at lunch and dinner, and longer evenings drinking imitation cognac and singing karaoke. For the foreign businessman with other things to do aside from behaving like a kindergarten kid during recess, this can be frustrating and irritating after the second day. Regardless of resources at hand, the foreign negotiating team is at the mercy of its Chinese hosts.

Although I estimate the troops of Tue as many, of what benefit is this superiority in terms of victory?

Thus, I say that victory can be achieved. For even if the enemy is numerically stronger, we can prevent him from fighting.

Therefore, analyse the enemy's battle plan, so as to have a clear understanding of its strong and weak points. Agitate the enemy, so as to ascertain his pattern of movement. Lure him into the open so as to find out his vulnerable spots in disposition. Probe him and learn where his strength is abundant and where deficient.

Many foreign multinationals simply refuse to conduct negotiations after an initial inspection visit of the Chinese party's factory, unless those negotiations are held in a "neutral location" specifically a five star hotel conference room in a coastal Chinese city. This way the foreign side can control the negotiation timing according to a schedule. Negotiations begin after breakfast, break at lunch, where both parties will have lunch separately. They will resume negotiations after lunch and conclude at a fixed time. After dinner there will be no partying as negotiations will be fixed to begin early the next morning. Only with such a structured program can any progress be made. At the end of the scheduled week of negotiations, the parties will then agree upon what has not yet been agreed upon, and before separating, fix a new time for further negotiations to commence. This will be done until the contract can be agreed and signed. This has proven to be the only way to conclude a deal, by controlling the opponent's environment. There is one catch however. Often the foreign side must foot the bill for the Chinese party's travel and hotel expenses to get them to sit at the table.

Now, the ultimate in disposing one's troops is to conceal them without ascertainable shape. In this way, the most penetrating spies cannot pry nor can the wise lay plans against you.

One example of such a situation was when an American multinational innocently told the Chinese party that his company wanted to be in full production by a certain date. The Chinese party simply dictated the terms from that point on. They gave the American party a standard Chinese contract which had nothing to do with the deal at hand.

When the foreign party questioned the document, the Chinese folded their arms and casually explained that it was what the foreign party had to do if they did in fact want to start production within their self-imposed time frame. The

Americans panicked and the Chinese had a field day at the negotiation table.

Even though we show people the victory gained by using flexible tactics in conformity to the changing situations, they do not comprehend this. People all know the tactics by which we achieved victory, but they do not know how the tactics were applied in the situation to defeat the enemy. Hence, no one victory is gained in the same as another. The tactics change in an infinite variety of ways to suit changes in the circumstances.

Negotiators coming to China with a fixed agenda, timetable or contracts are destined to be both disappointed and frustrated. An enormous amount of time is often spent by executives in conferences discussing negotiation strategies or drafting and redrafting contracts before even presenting those to the Chinese party. Much of this kind of effort is wasted, and for all practical purposes, achieves nothing except exhaustion before the executives even get to the negotiation table with their Chinese counterparts who will more often than not have completely different ideas.

Now, the laws of military operations are like water. The tendency of water is to flow from heights to lowlands. The law of successful operations is to avoid the enemy's strength and strike his weakness. Water changes its course in accordance with the contours of the land. The soldier works out his victory in accordance with the situation of the enemy. Hence, just as water retains no constant shape, so in war there are no constant conditions.

It is better to have a flexible approach, to observe carefully the attitudes of the Chinese side's negotiators, and to respond positively to situations in order to guide them to a closer position from which a compromise may be reached, rather than to come to the table with pre-fixed unattainable ideas.

He who can modify his tactics in accordance with the enemy situation and thereby succeed in winning may be said to be divine. Of the five elements, none is very predominant; of the four seasons, none lasts forever; of the days, some are longer and others shorter, and of the moon, it sometimes waxes and sometimes wanes.

CHAPTER 7

Manoeuvring

Sun Tzu advocated capitalizing on the indirect approach to resolve difficulties, that is, making the indirect approach the most direct. The Chinese refer to this as *bian tong ban fa* or "indirect approach." Negotiating in China offers many opportunities for adopting *bian tong ban fa*.

Due to China's own system, which for decades involved multiple layers of bureaucracy, approvals and regulations for most aspects of life, all Chinese have developed an intrinsic *bian tong ban fa* mentality, seeking the shortest route through red tape and the quickest way of avoiding any obvious problem.

SunTzu said: Normally, in war, the general receives his commands from the sovereign. During the process from assembling the troops and gathering the supplies to deploying the army ready for battle, nothing is more difficult than the art of manoeuvring for seizing favorable positions beforehand. What is difficult about it is to make the devious route the most direct and to turn disadvantage to advantage. Thus, forcing the enemy to deviate and slow down his march by luring him with a bait, you may set out after he does and arrive at the battle field before him. One able to do this shows the knowledge of artifice of deviation.

One day in the course of negotiations between Madame Wang, the Director of the Chinese party, commonly referred to as "dragon lady" Wang, and her favorite German corporate representative, she produced a pile of invoices and asked the German company to reimburse her.

Madame Wang explained that the expenses were for the traveling she undertook when checking the goods which she intended to return to the German company. Among the invoices was one for the purchase of three mangoes. The value on the invoice was an outrageous RMB160.

Thus, both advantage and danger are inherent in manoeuvring for an advantageous position. One who sets the entire army in motion with impedimenta to pursue an advantageous position will be too slow to attain it. If he abandons the camp and all the impedimenta to contend for advantage, the baggage and stores will be lost. It follows that when the army rolls up the armor and sets out speedily, stopping neither day nor night and marching at double speed for a hundred li to wrest an advantage, the commander of three divisions will be captured. The vigorous troops will arrive first and the feeble will straggle along behind, so that if this method is used only one-tenth of the army will arrive. In a forced march of fifty li the commander of the first and van division will fall, and using this method but half of the army will arrive. In a forced march of thirty li, but two-thirds will arrive. Hence, the army will be lost without baggage train; and it cannot survive without provisions, nor can it last long without sources of supplies.

The German representative asked Madame Wang why she was asking for reimbursement for purchasing three very overpriced mangoes. Madame Wang replied that she had bought the mangoes as a gift for the German representative, his colleague and another local colleague, Mr Chen, living in Beijing. Both the German representative and his colleague denied ever receiving the mangoes.

Madame Wang insisted that she had sent them to Mr Chen in Beijing. The German representative and his colleague then ran up long-distance telephone calls chasing after Mr. Chen to find out what had happened to their mangoes. Meanwhile, Madame Wang collected her reimbursement.

One who is not acquainted with the designs of his neighbors should not enter into alliances with them. Those who do not know the conditions of mountains and forests, hazardous defiles, marshes and swamps, cannot conduct the march of an army. Those who do not use local guides are unable to obtain the advantages of the ground. Now, war is based on deception. Move when it is advantageous and change tactics by dispersal and concentration of your troops. When campaigning, be as swift as the wind; in leisurely march, be as majestic as the forest; in raiding and plundering, be as fierce as fire; in standing, be as firm as the mountains. When hiding, be as unfathomable as things behind the clouds; when moving, fall like a thunderclap. When you plunder the countryside, divide your forces. When you conquer territory, defend strategic points. Weigh the situation before you move. He who knows the artifice of deviation will be victorious. Such is the art of manoeuvring.

When faced with an awkward situation, the Chinese will resort to deviation as opposed to head-on conflict. In this regard, the Chinese have a very flexible approach to handling problems when they arise and turning the situation around. One very colorful example of this occurred on China Southern Airlines, when the meal boxes were being passed out at lunch time during a flight.

China Southern Airlines is not particularly known for its meals or service. The meal boxes were cardboard boxes filled with assorted cakes and cookies, along with various scraps of meat bundled in tissue paper. The bottoms of most boxes had rotted through because of the grease oozing out of the meat. One gentleman opened the cardboard box, looked at the meat, then looked at the stewardess in perplexity, and asked, "Sorry Miss, do you have a Muslim 'Halal' meal?"

The Book of Army Management says: "As the voice cannot be heard in battle, gongs and drums are used. As troops cannot see each other clearly in battle, flags and banners are used." Now, gongs and drums, banners and flags are used to unify the action of the troops. When the troops can be thus united, the brave cannot advance alone, nor can the cowardly retreat. This is the art of directing large masses of troops. In night fighting, then, make much use of torches and drums; in day fighting, of flags and banners as a means of guiding the troops through their ears and eyes.

The China Southern Airlines stewardess took control of the situation. She snapped back the lid of the box before the astonished passenger's eyes, opened it, and punctured the paper bag of assorted meat with her red varnished fingernails. She lifted it out of the box and let the meat bundle slither off her fingernails onto the aluminum service cart with a plunk. She then graciously returned the box to the man, containing only cakes and cookies. "Your Muslim 'Halal' meal, Sir."

The man opened the box, looked at the cakes and cookies in bewilderment. He then began to nibble at a cookie—albeit with caution.

A whole army may be robbed of its spirit, and its commander deprived of his presence of mind. Now, at the beginning of a campaign, the spirit of soldiers is keen: after a certain period of time, it declines; and in the later stage, it may have dwindled to nought. A clever commander, therefore, avoids the enemy when his spirit is keen and attacks him when it is lost. This is the art of attaching importance to moods. In good order, he awaits a disorderly enemy; in serenity, a clamorous one.

Diversionary tactics are a key aspect of how the Chinese deal with uncomfortable situations or potential clashes of interest or view. Such diversionary tactics can best be analysed on a simple level, for instance, like the time when a Western businesswoman got violently sick eating in a local restaurant in Beijing.

The woman had gone into a small restaurant and ordered "doufu" thinking that it would be soft and easy to digest as a meal. When she returned to the hotel room, she was struck with one of the worst cases of Chiang Kaishek's "revenge" imaginable.

This is the art of retaining self-possession. Close to the field of battle, he awaits an enemy coming from afar: at rest, he awaits an exhausted enemy; with well-fed troops, he awaits hungry ones. This is the art of husbanding one's strength. He refrains from intercepting an enemy whose banners are in perfect order, and desists from attacking an army whose formations are in an impressive array. This is the art of assessing circumstances.

The next day the woman indignantly returned to the restaurant, found the owner, and reiterated her entire post-dinner experience, describing it in the most graphic of colors and arguing that it was the fault of the restaurant owner for not running a hygienic establishment.

The owner politely listened to her complaint. When she had finished, he responded in a soothing voice, "It's alright. Next time you come to eat at our restaurant, you do not have to choose the 'doufu.' We have lots of other dishes you can choose from instead."

Now, the art of employing troops is that when the enemy occupies high ground, do not confront him uphill, and when his back is resting on hills, do not make a frontal attack. When he pretends to flee, do not pursue. Do not attack soldiers whose temper is keen. Do not swallow a bait offered by the enemy. Do not thwart an enemy who is returning homewards. When you surround an army, leave an outlet free. Do not press a desperate enemy too hard. Such is the method of using troops.

CHAPTER 8

Variation of Tactics

Chinese culture places a premium on harmony. Open conflict is something to be avoided. When disputes arise in a contract, the Chinese always prefer to resolve them through amicable, non-binding conciliation talks between the parties rather than confrontation. While amicable dispute settlement will probably be frustrating, time-consuming and not altogther amicable, it is still the preferred means.

Sun Tzu said: Generally, in war, the general receives his commands from the sovereign to assemble his troops and gather the supplies. When on grounds hard of access, do not encamp. On grounds intersected with highways, join hands with your allies. Do not linger on critical ground. In encircled ground, resort to stratagem. In desperate ground, fight a last-ditch battle.

When a conflict becomes irreconcilable, there is no choice but to fight. However, one should always try to avoid reaching a deadlock in a negotiation, especially if one wants to keep the deal in motion. Therefore, it is best not to fall on desperate ground but instead, to resort to stratagems which will keep the deal in play.

There are some roads which must not be followed, some troops which must not be attacked, some cities which must not be assaulted, some ground which must not be contested, and some commands of the sovereign which must not be obeyed.

One Taiwanese businessman turned up at the office of his lawyers in Hong Kong to discuss his China joint venture contract. He complained when they served him tea, "Oh, this is 'mainland' tea. I cannot drink it. It is too strong and bitter to drink. I can only drink Taiwan tea, not this 'mainland' type."

Hence, the general who thoroughly understands the advantages that accompany variation of tactics knows how to employ troops. The general who does not is unable to use the terrain to his advantage even though he is well acquainted with it. In employing the troops for attack, the general who does not understand the variation of tactics will be unable to use them effectively, even if he is familiar with the Five Advantages.

The lawyer went into the pantry with the cup of tea. Turning to his secretary who had followed him there, he said in a loud voice, "Let's throw out this tea and give Mr Chu some of that wonderful Taiwan tea we have."

"But you know that all the tea here is from mainland China. We don't have any Taiwan tea," whispered the secretary.

"It doesn't matter. He will never know. Just give me another tea cup—one with a different colour." The lawyer then poured the same tea—now cold—into the new tea cup, returned to the conference room, and presented it to the Taiwanese businessman.

"Ah. This is much better!" exclaimed the Taiwanese businessman.

And for this reason, a wise general in his deliberations must consider both favorable and unfavorable factors. By taking into account the favorable factors, he makes his plan feasible; by taking into account the unfavorable, he may avoid possible disasters.

One example of a dispute being settled without a fight involved a US multinational applying pressure on several fronts: first negotiating with the Chinese partner, a shareholding company; then going to the shareholders themselves to exert pressure; then turning to the Ministry of Light Industry—the administrative organ above the company—and finally going to what was then the State Council Production Office to apply pressure downwards.

What can subdue the hostile neighboring rulers is to hit what hurts them most; what can keep them constantly occupied is to make trouble for them; and what can make them rush about is to offer them ostensible allurements.

As Sun Tzu's son, Sun Ping, once advised General Tian Chi, "To unravel a knot, you must not hold it tight. To settle a quarrel, you must not join in the fighting. If we leave what is knotted and attack what is loose, making further entanglement impossible, matters can be sorted out."

In this case, by applying government pressure to the shareholders of the Chinese partner, a behind-the-scenes but face-saving solution was found.

It is a doctrine of war that we must not rely on the likelihood of the enemy's not coming, but on our own readiness to meet him; not on the chance of his not attacking, but on the fact that we have made our position invincible.

Exploding at the negotiation table leads nowhere. In one rather dramatic negotiation, which degenerated into a screaming match, the foreign negotiation team leader kept shouting at his Chinese counterpart, "You are stupid. You are stupid. You don't realize that we have advanced technology and will help to modernize you!"

The Chinese negotiation team leader, in turn, hollered back, "You are unreasonable. You are insensitive to the Chinese situation. You ignore our laws."

Fortunately, the translators for both the Chinese and foreign teams refused to translate what was being said. Sensibly, they left the room to have a cigarette, leaving both negotiators screaming at each other, but unable to understand what the other was saying.

There are five dangerous faults which may affect a general: If reckless, he can be killed; if cowardly, he can be captured; if quick-tempered, he can be provoked to rage and make a fool of himself; if he has too delicate a sense of honor, he is liable to fall into a trap because of an insult; if he is of a compassionate nature, he may get bothered and upset. These are the five serious faults of a general, ruinous to the conduct of war. The ruin of the army and the death of the general are inevitable results of these five dangerous faults. They must be deeply pondered.

CHAPTER 9

On the March

Negotiating a China deal may seem like a "long march" for many. Patience is a classical Chinese virtue and one which has survived through the ages. When negotiating a China deal in China itself, one can better appreciate this unique aspect of Chinese culture and also gain some understanding as to why the Chinese place such a high premium on the virtue of patience. In China, patience is a basis for survival.

When one Hong Kong developer decided to try and negotiate over one of the neoclassic buildings along Shanghai's Bund, with the hope of turning it into a first-rate international bankers and financiers club, he learned that the Chinese were not as anxious as the developer expected to see this monument transformed.

Sun Tzu said: Generally, when an army takes up a position and sizes up the enemy situation, it should pay attention to the following:

When crossing the mountains, be sure to stay in the neighborhood of valleys; when encamping, select high ground facing the sunny side; when high ground is occupied by the enemy, do not ascend to attack. So much for taking up a position in mountains.

Negotiations began at the end of 1994. The Xin Ya Group adopted a tough position by telling the developer that the building was theirs. They claimed that they had managed it for dozens of years. The developer insisted on having management control as part of his conditions for the joint venture investment. The building at that time housed the "Seaman's Club" and was crawling with the lowest-class prostitutes to be picked out of the bowels of Shanghai's worst gutter. The Xin Ya Group argued back, "We have fine management. In fact, we export our management skills to the world."

After crossing a river, you should get far away from it. When an advancing invader crosses a river, do not meet him in midstream. It is advantageous to allow half his force to get across and then strike. If you wish to fight a battle, you should not go to meet the invader near a river which he has to cross. When encamping in the riverine area, take a position on high ground facing the sun. Do not take a position at the lower reaches of the enemy. This relates to positions near a river.

In January 1995, the Hong Kong developer was told that the Shanghai Bund Company (an organization established under the Shanghai Land and Housing commission for the purpose of leasing the old pre-liberation classical buildings on the Bund) had the rights over the building. On this basis, the Hong Kong developer would have to negotiate with the Shanghai Bund Company directly and not with the Xin Ya Group. He was told that the Xin Ya Group, in fact, was only a "user" of the building and the real "owner" was the Shanghai Bund Company.

The Hong Kong developer therefore dropped negotiations with the Xin Ya Group and began negotiations with the Shanghai Bund Company exclusively.

In crossing salt marshes, your sole concern should be to get over them quickly, without any delay. If you encounter the enemy in a salt march, you should take position close to grass and water with trees to your rear. This has to do with taking up a position in salt marshes.

In March 1995, negotiations began with the Shanghai Bund Company. They claimed that many developers were coming to them with proposals. "You have to give us your proposal. We are like a beautiful girl being courted. We can select this one. We can select that one. We may not select anyone. This is how we will discuss the project."

The developer went back and put together an expensive presentation for the project. Another developer did a model. Everybody went to Shanghai to discuss their proposals with the Shanghai Bund Company.

On level ground, take up an accessible position and deploy your main flanks on high ground with the front lower than the back. This is how to take up a position on level ground.

The Xin Ya Group was not to be beaten so easily. They responded with claims that they should be compensated and that they should be involved in the management of the building. The conflict between the Shanghai Bund Company and the Xin Ya Group was not over. The developers, however, were busy talking with the Shanghai Bund Company.

These are principles for encamping in the four situations named. By employing them, the Yellow emperor conquered his four neighboring sovereigns.

Meanwhile, the Hong Kong developer wanted to beat the four competing developers making proposals to the Shanghai Bund Company for the same building. In order to win local support from the municipal government authorities, in June of that year the developer held a luncheon at the Jin Jiang Hotel, and gave an expensive luncheon presentation to all departments of the Shanghai Municipal Government which would be required to support and approve the project. The Shanghai Bund Company representatives showed up late, and were embarrassed to find the former Communist Party Secretary of Shanghai attending. Everyone stood beside him for a photograph. Nobody from the Xin Ya Group attended.

Generally, in battle and manoeuvring, all armies prefer high ground to low, and sunny places to shady. If an army encamps close to water and grass with adequate supplies, it will be free from countless diseases and this will spell victory. When you come to hills, dikes, or embankments, occupy the sunny side, with your main flank at the back. All these methods are advantageous to the army and can exploit the possibilities the ground offers.

Following a successful presentation before the Shanghai Municipal Government authorities, the old Communist Party Secretary yelled at the Shanghai Bund Company for wasting so much time and ordered them to hurry up with discussions with the developer who had made such an elaborate presentation. The Shanghai Bund Company quickly called the developer in for a meeting.

During the meeting, the developer presented the entire elaborate presentation again for the Shanghai Bund Company. The Shanghai Bund Company informed the developer that a Southeast Asian development bank also wanted to invest in the project and that they favored that proposal instead. However, both contenders would be invited to give proposal talks again.

When heavy rain falls in the upper reaches of a river and foaming water descends, do not ford and wait until it subsides. In countries where there are "Precipitous Torrents," "Heavenly Wells," "Heavenly Prisons," "Heavenly Nets," "Heavenly Traps," and "Heavenly Cracks," you must march speedily away from them. Do not approach them. While we keep a distance from them we should draw the enemy toward them. We face them and cause the enemy to put his back to them. If you are near dangerous defiles or ponds and low-lying ground overgrown with aquatic grass and reeds, or forested mountains with dense and tangled undergrowth, they must be thoroughly searched, for these are possible places where ambushes are laid and spies are hidden.

The Hong Kong developer returned to give a presentation for the project at the Shanghai Bund Company. This presentation was given before officials from the Shanghai Planning Commission and the Shanghai Bureau of Cultural Relics Protection. The Southeast Asian development bank had made their presentation the day before. The Southeast Asian development bank, in the name of development, basically wanted to destroy the whole building, leaving only the old façade, and construct a high-rise building on the site. The Hong Kong developer wanted to entirely preserve the old building and to restore it to the style of the old Shanghai Club, which was originally housed in the building in the early 1900s.

The officials in the Shanghai Planning Commission and Shanghai Bureau of Cultural Relics Protection basically supported the Hong Kong developer's ideas as there already were enough skyscrapers going up in Shanghai. They told the

Shanghai Bund Company to support the restoration proposal of the Hong Kong developer. The end seemed near. In actual fact, this was only the beginning.

When the enemy is close at hand and remains quiet, he is relying on a natural stronghold. When he challenges battle from afar, he wishes to lure you to advance; when he is on easy ground, he must be in an advantageous position.

The Xin Ya Group then returned to the scene in August, claiming that they wanted to have the building turned over to them. In fact, they had made an application to the Shanghai Municipal Government to take the rights away from the Shanghai Bund Company and turn the rights over to them. The land title was now in question.

When the trees are seen to move, it means the enemy is advancing; when many screens have been placed in the undergrowth, it is for the purpose of deception. The rising of birds in their flight is the sign of an ambuscade. Startled beasts indicate that a sudden attack is forthcoming. Dust spurting upward in high straight columns indicates the approach of chariots. When it hangs low and is widespread, it betokens that infantries are approaching. When it branches out in different directions, it shows that parties have been sent out to collect firewood. A few clouds of dust moving to and fro signify that the army is camping.

In a meeting with the Shanghai Bund Company in October 1995, the Hong Kong developer was told that the land title was now in dispute between the Shanghai Bund Company and the Xin Ya Group. The Shanghai Bund Company explained that now that the developer's plans for the site had been accepted, he must be patient because it would take time to sort out this land title issue with the Xin Ya Group. Maybe he could invest in a resort outside of Shanghai? The Shanghai Bund Company had lots of other projects too—"all good and guaranteed to make money." The developer declined and decided to wait for news of the dispute.

When the enemy's envoys speak in humble terms, but the army continues preparations, that means it will advance. When their language is strong and the enemy pretentiously drives forward, these may be signs that he will retreat. When light chariots first go out and take positions on the wings, it is a sign that the enemy is forming for battle. When the enemy is not in dire straits but asks for a truce, he must be plotting. When his troops march speedily and parade informations, he is expecting to fight a decisive battle on a fixed date. When half his force advances and half retreats, he is attempting to decoy you.

In January 1996, the Shanghai Bund Company asked the Hong Kong developer to come to Shanghai to meet with them to discuss the situation relating to them as well as Xin Ya Group's claim over the land title. The developer flew to Shanghai. The Shanghai Bund Company never showed up. The developer then flew away and waited for news.

When he was next in Shanghai, the Shanghai Bund Company apologized for canceling the last meeting. They scheduled a new meeting first thing the next morning. Then they called to say that they were going to be late. Then they called to say that they could not arrive before lunch. They then called to say that they would come over to meet with the developer right after lunch. Then they called after lunch to say that they were going to be late. Then they stopped calling. They never showed up.

When his troops lean on their weapons, they are famished. When drawers of water drink before carrying it to camp, his troops are suffering from thirst. When the enemy sees an advantage but does not advance to seize it, he is fatigued. When birds gather above his camp sites they are unoccupied. When at night the enemy's camp is clamorous, it betokens nervousness. If there is disturbance in the camp, the general's authority is weak. If the banners and flags are shifted about, sedition is afoot.

In March 1996, the Shanghai Bund Company finally called the developer to have another meeting. They showed up this time. They announced gleefully that the land title issue had finally been solved and that the title would be theirs and not the Xin Ya Group's. But before going any further, the Shanghai Bund Company wanted to first negotiate how the profits would be shared between the parties. The Hong Kong developer said that this was an issue for concrete negotiations. The Shanghai Bund Company explained that they had to know how much they would get in order to consider whether or not to begin concrete negotiations. Needless to say, no progress was made on this issue.

The Hong Kong developer insisted as a condition that first, he must have clear confirmation that the Southeast Asian development bank was no longer competing for the project as he did not want to get into further negotiations if he was only being played off against the Southeast Asian development bank for a price. He was assured that their plan had been denied by the Shanghai Municipal government authorities concerned.

If the officers are angry, it means that they are weary. When the enemy feeds his horses with grain, kills the beasts of burden for food and packs up the utensils used for drawing water, he shows no inten-

tion to return to his tents and is determined to fight to the death. When the general speaks in meek and subservient tones to his subordinates, he has lost the support of his men. Too frequent rewards indicate that the general is at the end of his resources; too frequent punishments indicate that he is in dire distress. If the officers at first treat the men violently and later are fearful of them, it shows supreme lack of intelligence.

The Hong Kong developer, however, using a contact, made inquiries indirectly with the Southeast Asian development bank. The representative of the Southeast Asian development bank denied that their plan had not been accepted by the Shanghai Municipal authorities. In fact, he complained that they were waiting for approval, but the Shanghai Bund Company kept canceling the meetings.

When envoys are sent with compliments in their mouths, it is a sign that the enemy wishes for a truce. When the enemy's troops march up angrily and remain facing yours for a long time, neither joining battle nor withdrawing, the situation demands great vigilance and thorough investigation.

Finally, the Hong Kong developer returned to Shanghai to discuss the matter with the Shanghai Bund Company representative. The Company representative told him that none of these issues were real problems. The developer then asked him what the real problem was. The Shanghai bund Company representative explained that, "The real problem is now that the land title has been resolved in favor of the Shanghai Bund Company, the Xin Ya Group has no claim to the title."

In war, numbers alone confer no advantage. If one does not advance by force recklessly, and is able to concentrate his military power through a correct assessment of the enemy situation and enjoys full support of his men, that would suffice. He who lacks foresight and underestimates his enemy will surely be captured by him.

The Hong Kong developer suspected a trap. He asked, "I do not understand. I thought that the land title issue had been solved in favor of you guys. That's what we wanted. So what's the problem?"

"The Xin Ya Group would like to manage the club project as their compensation for not having won on the land title issue," explained the Shanghai Bund Company representative.

"That's impossible. Their management is terrible. We can only invest if we manage."

"Then you must go back and start talking to the Xin Ya Group to resolve this issue first," explained the Shanghai Bund Company representative. "We think that you should first go back and talk to the Xin Ya Group."

If troops are punished before they have grown attached to you they will be disobedient. If not obedient, it is difficult to employ them. If troops have become attached to you, but discipline is not enforced, you cannot employ them either. Thus, soldiers must be treated in the first instance with humanity, but kept under control by iron discipline. In this way, the allegiance of soldiers is assured. If orders are consistently carried out and the troops are strictly supervised, they will be obedient. If orders are never carried out, they will be disobedient. And the smooth implementation of orders reflects harmonious relationship between the commander and his troops.

CHAPTER 10

Terrain

Knowing the local situation is critical to negotiation success in China. Therefore, it should come as no surprise that more and more multinationals are hiring local staff, especially if they have foreign degrees, to help them weave between the intertwining complications of a China deal.

Sun Tzu said: Ground may be classified according to its nature as accessible, entangling, temporizing, constricted, precipitous and distant. Ground which both we and the enemy can traverse with equal ease is called accessible. On such ground, he who first takes the high and sunny side, and keeps his supply routes unimpeded can fight advantageously. Ground easy to reach but difficult to exit is called entangling.

During the process of submitting the relevant documents to the relevant authorities for joint venture approval, Mr Gao of the Chinese company, which was partner to the deal, did all of the running around between government offices to obtain the approval. When the project was finally approved, Mr Gao complained to the Managing Director of the foreign partner that he deserved an award for his hard work. In fact, he complained so much that the Managing Director of the foreign partner finally agreed to arrange a trip for Mr Gao to visit South Korea at the foreign company's cost, even though Mr. Gao was with the Chinese partner. Mr Gao later complained that he in fact did not want to go to South Korea at all. Instead, he would rather have the money for the value of such a trip. The Managing Director of the foreign partner finally gave Mr Gao some US$3,000—just to get rid of him.

The nature of this ground is such that if the enemy is unprepared and you sally out, you may defeat him. But, if the enemy is prepared for your coming, and you fail to defeat him, then, return being difficult, disadvantageous for both the enemy and ourselves to enter is called temporizing. The nature of this ground is such that even though the enemy should offer us an attractive bait, it will be advisable not to go forth but march off.

One should really take care in looking into the nature of one's Chinese business partner. A seemingly charismatic and energetic partner may not be an asset but a liability in disguise. The story of a Chinese–German joint venture manufacturing automobile parts and equipment in Shanghai is a case in point. The General Manager was appointed by the Chinese partner.

The General Manger pushed the foreign partner many times to put the capital investment into the joint venture in full. When the capital was finally paid in, that same General Manager's first business decision was to take the money out and use it to purchase four luxurious Santana automobiles for himself and his colleagues.

When his force is halfway out because of our manoeuvring we can strike him with advantage. With regard to the constricted ground, if we first occupy it, we must block the narrow passes with strong garrisons and wait for the enemy. Should the enemy first occupy such ground, do not attack him if the pass in his hand is fully garrisoned, but only if it is weakly garrisoned. With regard to the precipitous ground, if we first occupy it, we must take a position on the sunny heights and await the enemy.

One group of investors drove five hours through the countryside to negotiate at a rural State-owned enterprise. They arrived in the small town at midnight and put up at a local hotel.

At the crack of dawn, the Chairman of the State enterprise factory sent a car to collect them from the hotel and bring them to the factory for a breakfast meeting. The investors were heralded into a tiny dining room in the factory draped in red, where the Chairman of the factory and his management team sat waiting around a table piled high with cookies.

Breakfast began at 8:00 A.M. sharp with karaoke singing before a massive KTV screen. Karaoke singing lasted throughout breakfast. Everyone present had to sing their favorite song—that is if they had a favorite. All of the songs were in Mandarin. If they didn't have a favorite, the Chairman of the factory would pick one. Everyone had to sing whether they could read the Chinese characters or not. Breakfast was followed by lunch—immediately afterwards.

If he first occupies such ground, we should march off and do not attack him. When the enemy is situated at a great distance from us, and the terrain where the two armies deploy is similar, it is difficult to provoke battle and unprofitable to engage him. These are the principles relating to six different types of ground. It is the highest responsibility of the general to inquire into them with the utmost care.

Maotai drinking lasted throughout lunch. In fact, it got so bad that the translator for the foreign partner, who was a young Chinese, had to excuse himself from the whole fray and hide in the toilet. He refused to come out for fear that he would be forced to drink more.

After a huge banquet, the Chairman of the factory ordered that *jiaozi* (steamed dumplings) be served. Throughout the banquet, nobody could communicate because the translator was still hiding in the toilet. So all the foreigners continued to drink *maotai* and get drunk.

There are six situations that cause an army to fail. They are: flight, insubordination, fall, collapse, disorganization and rout. None of these disasters can be attributed to natural and geographical causes, but to the fault of the general. Terrain conditions being equal, if a force attacks one ten times its size, the result is flight. When the soldiers are strong and officers weak, the army is insubordinate. When the officers are valiant and the soldiers ineffective, the army will fall. When the higher officers are angry and insubordinate, and on encountering the enemy rush to battle on their own account from a feeling of resentment and the commander-in-chief is ignorant of their abilities, the result is collapse.

Because the young translator refused to come out of the toilet, the Chairman of the factory ordered his staff to bring plates of *jiaozi* into the toilet to force the young translator to eat there if he would not come out to eat and drink at the table with him, giving him *mianzi* ("face").

Finally, the translator obediently returned to the table. The Chairman of the factory got his "face." By this time, all the foreigners on the negotiating team were sick.

When the general is incompetent and has little authority, when his troops are mismanaged, when the relationship between the officers and men is strained, and when the troop formations are slovenly, the result is disorganization.

Nothing was discussed that afternoon—in the one and a half hours reserved for constructive talks. During the discussions, nothing could be resolved and the investors were too exhausted to pursue any kind of concentrated effort.

"No problem," exclaimed the Chairman of the factory with glee. He had arranged for a banquet with local government officials in the evening—starting at 5:00 P.M. sharp!

When a general unable to estimate the enemy's strength uses a small force to engage a larger one or weak troops to strike the strong, or he fails to select shock troops for the van, the result is rout. When any of these six situations exists, the army is on the road to defeat. It is the highest responsibility of the general that he examines them carefully.

Finding the right ground in China is half the challenge. One foreign investment enterprise worked very hard to try and negotiate with a chemical factory which could not decide whether or not it wanted to produce its products in the existing factory or to develop a Greenfield site. Finally, after sending technicians to the site over a period of a year, the multinational's headquarters decided that they should build the Greenfield site and not renovate the existing factory. It then came to their attention that if they built the Greenfield project, the Chinese partner would have nothing to contribute as part of their equity.

Confirmation of the ground is of great assistance in military opera-
tions. It is necessary for a wise general to make correct assessments of
the enemy's situation to create conditions leading to victory and to
calculate distances and the degree of difficulty of the terrain. He who
knows these things and applies them to fighting will definitely win.
He who knows them not, and, therefore, is unable to apply them, will
definitely lose.

Because of the sensitivity of this particular chemical industry, it was impossible for the foreign partner to establish a wholly owned enterprise without a Chinese partner. Consequently,
to proceed with the same partner with whom they had negoti-
ated for over a year, they would need to pay the Chinese partner cash to become a part of the joint venture so that the
Chinese partner would have something to contribute as its
equity. As expected, this concept was also not acceptable to the
multinational's headquarters.

Hence, if, in the light of the prevailing situation, fighting is sure to
result in victory, then you may decide to fight even though the sov-
ereign has issued an order not to engage. If fighting does not stand a
good chance of victory, you need not fight even though the sovereign
has issued an order to engage. Hence, the general who advances with-
out coveting fame and retreats without fearing disgrace, whose only
purpose is to protect his people and promote the best interests of his
sovereign, is the precious jewel of the State.

One Taiwanese working for a foreign multinational was
assigned to be the General Manger of a joint venture which was
in a small town in Hubei Province. This General Manager,
however, wanted to live in a luxurious villa in Shanghai and
have a driver and entertainment expenses to boot. He talked

himself into a job with the foreign company on the basis that being from Taiwan, he spoke Mandarin, and would therefore be best suited to "interact with the Chinese" because he was "Chinese too." He then went to the small town in Hubei, which was the site of the joint venture, and told the Chinese partner the same thing.

If a general regards his men as infants, then they will march with him into the deepest valleys. He treats them as his own beloved sons and they willingly die with him. If, however, a general is indulgent towards his men but cannot employ them, cherishes them but cannot command them or inflict punishment on them when they violate the regulations, then they may be compared to spoiled children and are useless for any practical purpose.

The problem was, this Taiwanese Manager established a routine that he would leave Shanghai on Monday morning, arrive in Wuhan on Monday night, spend the night in a four-star hotel in Wuhan, and then on Tuesday morning depart for the factory, arriving Tuesday afternoon. He would then work there all day Wednesday, and start preparations for returning to Shanghai on Thursday.

Despite his verbal claims that he loved China and working with the Chinese and his touted communications skills, it was obvious to the Chinese partner that he did not want to be there working with them. They finally complained to his superior from headquarters. Headquarters later appointed a German Manager to work in the factory. The Taiwanese Manager insisted that as "Regional Asia-Pacific Manager" he should move his own office to Hong Kong so as to be closer to the rest of Asia and the Pacific as well!

If we know that our troops are capable of striking the enemy, but do not know that he is invulnerable to attack, our chance of victory is but half. If we know that the enemy is vulnerable to attack but do not know that our troops are incapable of striking him, our chance of victory is again but half. If we know that the enemy can be attacked and that our troops are capable of attacking him, but do not realize that the conformation of the ground makes fighting impracticable, our chance of victory is once again but half. Therefore, when those experienced in war move, they are never bewildered; when they act, they are never at a loss. Thus the saying: Know the enemy and know yourself, and your victory will never be endangered; know the weather and know the ground, and your victory will then be complete.

CHAPTER 11

The Nine Varieties of Ground

Sun Tzu believed that an understanding of conditions was critical for success when entering unfamiliar ground. The successful strategist first makes the unfamiliar known and understood before penetrating deeper.

Likewise, in entering a China negotiation, knowing your ground is critical for success. That is why many multinationals hire consultants, so-called "China hands," or Chinese who claim to be the sons and daughters of State leaders.

Sun Tzu said: In respect of the employment of troops, ground may be classified as dispersive, frontier, key, open, focal, serious, difficult, encircled, and desperate. When a chieftain is fighting in his own territory, he is in dispersive ground. When he has penetrated into hostile territory, but to no great distance, he is in frontier ground. Ground equally advantageous for us and the enemy to occupy is key ground. Ground equally accessible to both sides is open.

It is the dream of every investor coming to China to find the all-time fixer, the son or daughter of some mysterious State leader, who has all the keys to all the doors. Such people exist only as a figment of others' imaginations. There is no single fixer who can fix everything. Nevertheless, if you are a Chinese collegiate or graduate student in America, just find a multinational and tell them that you are the nephew of Deng Xiaoping or a niece of Jiang Zemin and a job will be waiting for you without question.

Ground contiguous to three other states is focal. He who first gets control of it will gain the support of the majority of neighboring states. When an army has penetrated deep into hostile territory, leaving far behind many enemy cities and towns, it is in serious ground. Mountain forests, rugged steppes, marshes, fens and all that is hard to traverse fall into the category of difficult ground. Ground to which access is constricted and from which we can only retire by tortuous paths so that a small number of the enemy would suffice to crush a large body of our men is encircled ground. Ground on which the army can avoid annihilation only through a desperate fight without delay is called a desperate one.

One Chinese lawyer who studied in a summer program at Columbia University, returned to China telling foreign law firms that she was the granddaughter of Marshal Ye Jianying. She went on to get a job at a prestigious Hong Kong law firm. She also spoke Cantonese. She began to dress in style and tell people in China that she was from Hong Kong. Eventually, when she proved that she could not do any work, she was fired.

She then went on to a smaller law firm, got a job as their Chief Representative on the pretense of her contacts, and began to blow the firm's office budget entertaining her friends on the basis that she needed to "keep up the contacts" for the firm. After she blew the budget altogether, she was also dismissed.

And, therefore, do not fight in dispersive ground; do not stop in the frontier borderlands. Do not attack an enemy who has occupied key ground; in open ground, do not allow your communication to be blocked. In focal ground, form alliances with neighboring states; in serious ground, gather in plunder. In difficult ground, press on; in encircled ground, resort to stratagems; and in desperate ground, fight courageously.

The girl then managed to entice the senior partner of an Australian law firm to bed, and he subsequently hired her to set up their Beijing representative office. She served as his mistress on his trips to Beijing and worked as the Chief Representative. The Australian partner then went back to Australia. The girl rented an expensive office in a five-star hotel, spent money on clothes, and eventually that office had to close as well. She explained that the failure of the office was all the fault of the Chinese government, communism and bureaucracy. The Australian law firm partner eventually fired her, disappointed that all her so-called powerful contacts in China did not come with the package.

In ancient times, those described as skilled in war knew how to make it impossible for the enemy to unite his van and his rear, for his large and small divisions to cooperate, for his officers and men to support each other, and for the higher and lower levels of the enemy to estab-lish contact with each other. When the enemy's forces were dispersed, they prevented him from assembling them; even when assembled, they managed to throw his forces into disorder. They moved forward when it was advantageous to do so; when not advantageous, they halted. Should one ask: "How do I cope with a well-ordered enemy host about to attack me?" I reply: "Seize what he cherishes and he will confirm to your desires."

As one prostitute working in the Palace Hotel in Beijing used to say about her Hong Kong and Taiwanese clients: "If you grab them by the balls, their hearts and minds will follow."

Speed is the essence of war. Take advantage of the enemy's unpreparedness, make your way by unexpected routes, and attack him where he has taken no precautions.

There is the story about a Hainanese who went to Canada. He sold himself to a company which had mining and wood pulp processing interests. He told them that he had many contacts in China and could "do anything." He then returned to Beijing and told officials there that he owned "gold mines in Canada" and wanted to bring his partners to China for investments. The officials opened their arms. He brought the Canadians. They received VIP treatment at the airport and stayed in the Diaoyutai State Guest House. They committed funds. The Chinese believed in them. Everyone believed in the Hainanese.

The general principles applicable to an invading force are that the deeper you penetrate into hostile territory, the greater will be the solidarity of your troops, and thus the defenders cannot overcome you. Plunder fertile country to supply your army with plentiful food. Pay attention to the soldiers' well-being and not fatigue them. Try to keep them in high sprits and conserve their energy. Keep the army moving and devise unfathomable plans. Throw your soldiers into a position whence there is no escape, and they will choose death over desertion. For if prepared to die, how can the officers and men not exert their uttermost strength to fight? In a desperate situation, they fear nothing; when there is no way out, they stand firm.

Time went on. Projects did not materialize. Nevertheless, the Hainanese on the back of his "gold mines" in Canada got to see one State leader after another in China. He then used photographs to lure investment claiming that he was very close to all of these leaders. The investors followed. More leaders came out to receive them.

Deep in a hostile land they are bound together. If there is no help for it, they will fight hard. Thus, without waiting to be marshaled, the soldiers will be constantly vigilant; without waiting to be asked, they will do your will; without restrictions, they will be faithful; without giving orders they can be trusted. Prohibit superstitious, practices and do away with rumors, then nobody will flee even facing death.

At the same time, nobody knew who the Hainanese was. In fact, nobody wanted to question who he was or even raise the specter of doubt in their minds. "I think he must be a relative of Deng Xiaoping," commented one serious investor. "Otherwise how could he have contacts with so many State leaders?" However, these investors who were normally so concerned about doing due diligence with projects, were all afraid to ask who this Hainanese was. "There are some things that are best not ask and best not to know," commented another serious believing investor.

Our soldiers have no surplus of wealth, but it is not because they disdain riches; they have no expectation of long life, but it is not because they dislike longevity. On the day the army is ordered out to battle, your soldiers may weep, those sitting up wetting their garments, and those lying down letting the tears run down their cheeks. But throw them into a situation where there is no escape and they will display the immortal courage of Zhuan Zhu and Cao Kuei.

Gaining ground in China may be difficult, on the one hand. On the other, it may not be as difficult as it seems. Many investors are busy trying to arrange for the CEOs of their big multinationals, to meet Jiang Zemin, Li Peng or Zhu Rongji hoping to access ground into the China market by using force from the top. This, however, is not the only way to gain ground. Working from the ground up may sometimes prove more effective.

Troops directed by a skilful general are comparable to the Shuai Ran. The Shuai Ran is a snake found in Mount Chang. Strike at its head, and you will be attacked by its tail; strike at its tail, and you will be attacked by its head; strike at its middle, and you will be attacked by both its head and its tail. Should one ask: "Can troops be made capable of such instantaneous coordination as the Shuai Ran?" I reply: "They can." For the men of Wu and the men of Yue are enemies, yet if they are crossing a river in the same boat and are caught by a storm, they will come to each other's assistance just as the left hand helps the right. Hence, it is not sufficient to rely upon tethering of the horses and the burying of the chariots.

Getting close to Chinese officials may not be as difficult as one may think. One American businessman who wanted to get close to a provincial Party Secretary showed up at a local agricultural exhibition where he knew that the provincial Party Secretary would be making a speech. As the officials lined up on the podium for the speech, the American businessman went to the podium as well and stood beside the Party Secretary.

The principle of military administration is to achieve a uniform level of courage. The principle of terrain application is to make the best use of both the high and the low-lying grounds. Thus, a skilful general conducts his army just as if he were leading a single man, willy-nilly, by the hand.

The businessman acted as if he himself was a special VIP official, and the Chinese were so impressed by a foreign visitor who appeared to be in an official capacity attending that they gave him special deference from the podium. He stood beside the Party Secretary, and greeted him very nicely. The Party Secretary also smiled and posed for photographs with the foreign businessman.

It is the business of a general to be calm and thus ensure depth in deliberation; impartial and upright, and thus keep a good management. He should be able to mystify his officers and men by false reports and appearances, and thus keep them in total ignorance. He changes his arrangements and alters his plans in order to make others unable to see through his strategies. He shifts his campsites and undertakes marches by devious routes so as to make it impossible for others to anticipate his objective. He orders his troops for a decisive battle on a fixed date and cuts off their return routes, as if he kicks away the ladder behind the soldiers when they have climbed up a height. When he leads his army deep into hostile territory, their momentum is trigger-released in battle. He burns his boats and breaks his cooking pots; he drives his men now in one direction, then in another, like a shepherd driving a flock of sheep, and no one knows where he is going. To assemble the host of his army and bring it into dangerous situations—this may be termed the business of the general. The different measures appropriate to the nine varieties of ground and the expediency of advance or withdrawal in accordance with circumstances and the fundamental laws of human nature are matters that must be studied carefully by a general.

As the Party Secretary toured the exhibition grounds looking at the various exhibits by the different agricultural companies and enterprises, this foreign businessman walked along beside him the whole time. The Party Secretary was taken unawares. Throughout the walk, they were being photographed and videotaped by television cameras and reporters. The Party Secretary relished the press he was receiving, partly stimulated by the presence of the foreign guest beside him.

Generally, when invading a hostile territory, the deeper the troops penetrate, the more cohesive they will be; penetrating only a short way causes dispersion. When you leave your own country behind, and take your army across neighboring territory, you find yourself on critical ground. When there are means of communication on all four sides, it is focal ground. When you penetrate deeply into a country, it is serious ground. When you penetrate but a little way, it is frontier ground. When you have the enemy's strongholds on your rear, and narrow passes in front, it is encircled ground. When there is no place of refuge at all, it is desperate ground.

Now the Party Secretary could not ignore the foreign businessman. He had become integral to the show. The Party Secretary could only let him get closer. They were soon exchanging cards.

Therefore, in dispersive ground, I would unify the determination of the army. In frontier ground, I would keep my forces closely linked. In key ground, I would hasten up my rear elements. In open ground, I would pay close attention to my defense. In focal ground, I would consolidate my alliances.

The Party Secretary was so happy to have a foreigner beside him, demonstrating his international contacts, that he posed at every point and exhibit at the show. For this reason, he was happy to have many photographs taken with the businessman.

In serious ground, I would ensure a continuous flow of provisions. In difficult ground, I would press on over the road. In encircled ground, I would block the points of access and egress. In desperate ground, I would make it evident that there is no chance of survival. For it is the nature of soldiers to resist when surrounded, to fight hard when there is no alternative, and to follow commands implicitly when they have fallen into danger.

As they progressed together around the exhibition grounds, the foreign businessman gradually began to explain what company he was with, passing brochures to the Party Secretary, explaining the project which his company was seeking to do in the province, and explaining the problems they were having in doing the project and getting approvals, and basically getting full support from the Party Secretary.

One ignorant of the designs of neighboring states cannot enter into alliance with them; if ignorant of the conditions of mountains, forests, dangerous defiles, swamps, and marshes, he cannot conduct the march of an army; if he fails to make use of native guides, he cannot gain the advantages of the ground. An army does not deserve the title of the invincible Army of the Hegemonic King if its commander is ignorant of even one of these nine varieties of ground. Now, when such an invincible army attacks a powerful state, it makes it impossible for the enemy to assemble his forces. It overawes the enemy and prevents his allies from joining him.

When it came time for the party Secretary to sit down at a show being held in the exhibition, he invited the foreign businessman to sit beside him, now in an official capacity. Knowing that the Party Secretary would be visiting Europe on another matter, the foreign businessman invited him to visit his company's headquarters and promised to fly to Europe to accompany the Party Secretary, who was overwhelmed with the apparent honor and agreed.

It follows that one does not need to seek alliances with other neighboring states, nor is there any need to foster the power of other states, but only to pursue one's own strategic designs to overawe his enemy. Then one can take the enemy's cities and overthrow the enemy's state.

One European company which had their entire deal almost tied up with a local partner, thought it best to still have a national-level partner involved for "government support." Despite advice to the contrary, they gave 5 percent of their equity to a company established under the ministry concerned with the industrial sector they were investing in.

Bestow rewards irrespective of customary practice and issue orders irrespective of convention, and you can command a whole army as though it were but one man. Set the troops to their tasks without revealing your designs. When the task is dangerous, do not tell them its advantageous aspect. Throw them into a perilous situation and they will survive; put them in desperate ground and they will live. For when the army is placed in such a situation, it can snatch victory from defeat.

To the surprise of the investors, this company under the ministry concerned, whom they were so graciously giving 5 percent of their equity to for nothing, suddenly became greedy. The company demanded a seat on the board of directors as well as management authority and greater guaranteed profits. The company threatened to jeopardize the deal if they did not get their own way.

Now, the key to military operations lies in cautiously studying the enemy's designs. Concentrate your forces in the main direction against the enemy and from a distance of a thousand li you can kill his general. This is called the ability to achieve one's aim in an artful and ingenious manner.

In the end, the investors had to fly to Beijing for meetings with the ministry itself in order to lobby the ministry to get rid of the company which was creating problems—the same company to whom they had given 5 percent equity—so as to have a line of access to the ministry for support. Finally, the ministry intervened and pulled their own company out of the deal at the request of the investors.

Therefore, on the day the decision is made to launch war, you should close the passes, destroy the official tallies, and stop the passage of all emissaries. Examine the plan closely in the temple council and make final arrangements. If the enemy leaves a door open, you must rush in. Seize the place the enemy values without making an appointment for battle with him. Be flexible and decide your line of action according to the situation on the enemy side. Then exhibit the coyness of a maiden until the enemy gives you an opening; afterwards be swift as a running hare, and it will be too late for the enemy to oppose you.

CHAPTER 12

Attack by Fire

In the West, we talk of "fighting fire with fire." This comes from the "eye for an eye" approach, which has become the basis of all Western legal systems and the advocacy approach of Western lawyers.

"You are not enough of an advocate!" screamed the French Financial Controller. "I want a real advocate!"

The next thing the French Financial Controller knew was that the waitress in the hotel was delivering a basket of frito-style chips from the hotel lobby bar. "What is this?" asked the French Financial Controller. "The waitress thought you said 'avocado' and figured you wanted to have some taco chips to go along with the guacamole," responded the lawyer.

> *Sun Tzu said: There are five ways of attacking with fire. The first is to burn soldiers in their camp; the second, to burn provisions and stores; the third, to burn baggage trains; the fourth, to burn arsenals and magazines; and the fifth, to burn the lines of transportation. To use fire, some medium must be relied upon. Materials for setting fire must always be at hand. There are suitable seasons to attack with fire, and special days for starting a conflagration. The suitable*

seasons are when the weather is very dry; the special days are those when the moon is in the constellations of the Sieve, the Wall, the Wing or the Cross-bar; for when the moon is in these positions there are likely to be strong winds all day long.

Many Western lawyers believe in being tough when dealing with their Chinese counterparts. "We have to be tough," explained one legal counsel for a big American multinational. To make his point clear, he wrote letter after letter to the Chinese side, setting forth and arguing his positions. The Chinese, however, never responded. The lawyer got more and more frustrated. He wrote even more letters.

Now, in attacking with fire, one must respond to the five changing situations: When fire breaks out in the enemy's camp, immediately coordinate your action from without. If there is an outbreak of fire, but the enemy's soldiers remain calm, bide your time and do not attack. When the force of the flames has reached its height, follow it up with an attack, if that is practicable; stay where you care, if not. If fires can be raised from outside the enemy's camps, it is not necessary to wait until they are started inside. Attack with fire only when the moment is suitable. If the fire starts from upwind, do not launch an attack from downwind. When the wind continues blowing during the day, it is likely to die down at night. Now, the army must know the five different fire attack situations and wait for appropriate times.

One of the main difficulties here is the disparity of systems. Where the foreign lawyer is being paid upwards of US$200 per hour to write letters to the Chinese, the Chinese are being paid less than US$100 per month to read them. Most do not bother. Some do bother to file the letters. Others use them to roll vegetables in to carry home after work on their bicycles.

Those who use fire to assist their attacks can achieve tangible results; those who use inundations can make their attacks more powerful. Water can intercept and isolate an enemy, but cannot deprive him of the supplies or equipment.

"We expect to have a reply to this letter at your earliest convenience," wrote the American legal counsel with irritation. No reply.

"We expect to have a response from you on this matter shortly," wrote the American legal counsel less patiently. No reply.

"We expect to have an immediate response from you if you expect us to believe that you are going to take this matter seriously," wrote the American legal counsel with even less patience than before. Still no reply.

Now, to win battles and capture lands and cities, but to fail to consolidate these achievements is ominous and may be described as a waste of resources and time. And, therefore, the enlightened rulers must deliberate upon the plans to go to battle, and good generals carefully execute them; if not in the interests of the state, do not act.

"If you do not respond immediately to our demands, we will raise this issue with the US Embassy in Beijing," wrote the American legal counsel in complete frustration.

If you are not sure of success, do not use troops. If you are not in danger, do not fight a battle. A sovereign should not launch a war simply out of anger, nor should a general fight a battle simply out of resentment.

Finally, the Chinese side replied, "Thank you for write letter. Please welcome to come China for make invest. Give best wishes to your family. Bring money."

Take action if it is to your advantage; cancel the action if it is not. An angered man can become happy again, just as a resentful one can feel pleased again, but a state that has perished can never revive, nor can a dead man be brought back to life. Therefore, with regard to the matter of war, the enlightened ruler is prudent, and the good general is full of caution. Thus, the state is kept secure and the army preserved.

CHAPTER 13

Use of Spies

Corporate espionage is a critical element behind every negotiation. Do not expect as you sit in the back seat of the car discussing the day's events that the driver assigned by the other side to shuttle you around does not understand English. Do not assume that the negotiators on the other side, who appear to rely so much on translators, do not either.

> *Sun Tzu said: Generally, when an army of one hundred thousand is raised and dispatched on a distant war, the expenses borne by the people together with the disbursements made by the treasury will come to an immense amount of money each day. There will be continuous commotion both at home and abroad; people will be involved with convoys and exhausted from performing transportation services, and seven hundred thousand households will be unable to continue their framework.*

The Chinese party will be aware that all this negotiating is costing the foreign side money. When the money does not bring results, they will realize that repercussions come with the problems. They will seek to find divisions in the foreign side.

Hostile armies confront each other for years in order to struggle for victory in a decisive battle; yet if one who begrudges the expenditure of rewards in honors and emoluments remains ignorant of his enemy's situation, he is completely devoid of humanity. Such a man is no leader of the troops; no capable assistance to his sovereign; no master of victory.

One feisty Chairman of an enterprise, when hosted in Europe by the foreign side, recognized divisions amongst the foreign side's managers. He asked one to meet with him in a private meeting during which he bad-mouthed the others on the foreign negotiation team. Then he asked the others to meet with him and said nice things. Then everybody on the foreign negotiation team fought amongst themselves and the negotiation stalled further, to the Chairman's own advantage.

Now, the reasons that the enlightened sovereign and the wise general conquer the enemy whenever they move and their achievements surpass those of ordinary men is that they have foreknowledge. This "foreknowledge" cannot be elicited from spirits, nor from gods, nor by analogy with past events, nor by any deductive calculations. It must be obtained from the men who know the enemy situation.

Consequently, foreign companies are willing to expend vast sums of money in undertaking market surveys before entering into negotiations in China. For example, one company spent US$100,000 a shot for management consultants to undertake these market surveys. Another company simply telephoned the Industrial Bureau in China concerned who just gave them the same information, since it had been published in their own industrial bureau publication.

Hence, the use of spies, of whom there are five sorts: native spies, internal spies, converted spies, doomed spies, and surviving spies. When all these five sorts of spies are at work and no one knows their method of operation, it would be divinely intricate and constitutes the greatest treasure of a sovereign. Native spies are those we employ from the enemy's country people. Internal spies are enemy officials whom we employ. Converted spies are enemy spies whom we employ. Doomed spies are those of our own spies who are deliberately given false information and told to transmit it to enemy spies. Surviving spies are those who return from the enemy camp to report information.

The most dangerous person is the driver. He knows where the boss goes and what the boss does. He knows his pattern and his disposition. One company executive invited another company executive to lunch in China. Meanwhile, the driver of the executive chatted with the driver of the other executive and gained more information about their company's activities in China than his boss was able to get over the luncheon with the other executive. "I know everything," bragged the driver. "I see all these executives come and go."

Hence, of all those in the army close to the commander, none is more intimate than the spies; of all rewards, none more liberal than those given to spies; of all matters, none is more confidential than those relating to spying operations. He who is not sage cannot use spies. He who is not humane and generous cannot use spies. And he who is not delicate and subtle cannot get the truth out of them. Delicate indeed! Truly delicate! There is no place where espionage is not possible. If plans relating to spying operations are prematurely divulged, the spy and all those to whom he spoke of them should be put to death.

When an old messenger from one foreign representative office went to deliver papers to a competitor, he sat down in the office and told the receptionist all about the internal problems of his employer. He thought he was smart and even told the receptionist that he was "advisor to the Chief Representative" in his capacity as a messenger. He was somehow looking for rewards from the other side. What he did not realize was that the receptionist was already working as counter-espionage for his employer. Before he arrived back at the office, she called the employer and told him everything she had heard. He fired the messenger upon his return to the office.

Generally, whether it be armies that you wish to strike, cities that you wish to attack, or individuals that you wish to assassinate, it is necessary to find out the names of the garrison commander, the aides-de-camp, the ushers, gatekeepers, and bodyguards. You must instruct your spies to ascertain these matters in minute detail.

One foreign businessman was so convinced that he was going to find bugs in his old, cavernous, Soviet-style hotel room that he searched everywhere, but to no avail. Finally, under the old red carpet, he found a metal plate with three screws holding it to the ground. Thrilled, he took a coin out of his pocket and unscrewed the first screw. Then he unscrewed the second screw. He was shaking with excitement at finding the bug when he had the third screw out, only to hear the old Russian chandelier crash down on the floor below.

It is essential to seek out enemy spies who have come to conduct espionage against you and bribe them to serve you. Courteously exhort them and give your instructions, then release them back home. Thus, converted spies are recruited and used. It is through the information brought by the converted spies that native and internal spies can be recruited and employed. It is owing to their information again, that the doomed spies, armed with false information, can be sent to convey it to the enemy. Lastly, it is by their information that the surviving spies can come back and give information as scheduled. The sovereign must have full knowledge of the activities of the five sorts of spies. And to know these depends upon the converted spies. Therefore, it is mandatory that they be treated with the utmost liberality.

If you want to know everything about your competitor's business in China, just hire his staff. Pay a little more and they will come over to your company. But beware, your competitor may pay just a little more and they will go over to the other side. In order to keep them from going to yet another competitor, you will have to continue to pay and pay and pay and pay.

In ancient times, the rise of the Shang Dynasty was due to Yi Zhi, who had served under the Xia. Likewise, the rise of the Zhou Dynasty was due to Lu Ya, who had served under the Yin. Therefore, it is only the enlightened sovereign and the wise general who are able to use the most intelligent people as spies and achieve great results. Spying operations are essential in war; upon them the army relies to make its every move.

Appendices

Appendix I

Brief History of Sun Tzu's Art of War

There is little known about the life of Sun Tzu. It is known that such a philosopher lived during the Spring and Autumn Period around 500 B.C.

It is also known that Sun Tzu had a son named Sun Ping, who later became a master strategist in his own right. Sun Ping is not discussed in this book, as his wisdom and thoughts are being saved for a future publication in the "Zhishangtan-bing" series.

The purpose of this Appendix is to summarize certain aspects of Sun Tzu's life and to draw relevance between the past and the present. This is intended to provide some background for readers unfamiliar with the text or historic background of Sun Tzu's Art of War.

Given that little is known about the life of Sun Tzu, the author has had to draw some rather broad and discretionary conclusions from the various existing historical reference materials and remaining ancient texts written in classical Chinese.

For those readers who feel that this brief summary of Sun

Tzu himself is incomplete, inaccurate, or does not provide adequate coverage of the subject matter, it is recommended that they take the time to delve into the various existing historical reference materials and remaining ancient texts written in classical Chinese.

Some of these can be found in the State-run museums of ancient and fabled historical cities, such as Xian and Loyang. There are even more ancient remnants of similar texts in the more remote cities of Lanzhou and Jingsha.

525 B.C.
Sun Tzu was born under the name of Sun Wu. The character "Tzu" is a title and means "Master" (as in "Grasshopper asks Master about the secrets of Kung Fu"). Sun Tzu therefore means "Master Sun." "Grasshopper" is also not a real name.

512 B.C.
Sun Wu writes the Art of War, sometimes translated as the Art of Strategy. It becomes a bestseller. After favorable reviews, Sun Wu becomes known as Sun Tzu.

510 B.C.
Sun Tzu meets the King of Wu and listens to his problems (see Appendix II for details).

500 B.C.
Sun Ping follows in the footsteps of his father Sun Tzu and uses many of the strategies in his father's Art of War.

A.D. 221
The first emperor, Qin Shi Huangdi, uses the Art of War to defeat the rival kingdoms. He also unifies China, and builds the

Great Wall to keep enemies out (the strategy of building the Great Wall is not, however, in Sun Tzu's Art of War).

A.D. 231

Cao Cao, one of the famous warrior-generals of the Three Kingdoms period, was the first person to explain, with notes, Sun Tzu's Art of War. Many of Cao Cao's own exploits are featured in the book When Yes Means No (or yes or maybe): How to Negotiate a Deal in China, also published by Tuttle Publishing, in 2003.

A.D. 242

Zhu Ge Liang, another famous strategist during the Three Kingdoms period, also supported the strategies in Sun Tzu's Art of War. Zhu Ge Liang believed that all strategies in war, one way or another, were derived from Sun Tzu's Art of War and that there were no strategic theories as broad and profound as Sun Tzu's..

A.D. 1798

The Art of War was translated by a French missionary who gives it to an upstart young general named Napoleon. It was reportedly studied and effectively employed by Napoleon, who became so loved by the French people that they named a sweet pastry dish after him.

A.D. 1812

Napoleon is defeated at the battle of Waterloo by a British general named Wellington who also read the Art of War. As a result, French artistic, cultural, and culinary influence over Britain is denied (Britain suffers from this loss for the next 190 years). In order to celebrate Wellington's successful use of the

Art of War, the British people named a heavy beef dish after him, "Beef Wellington."

A.D. 1949

Mao Zedong uses Sun Tzu's Art of War to defeat both the Japanese and the Kuomintang. Mao incorporates some of Sun Tzu's strategies into his own book of strategies, later published in abridged form during the Cultural Revolution as *The Red Book*. It becomes an immediate bestseller.

A.D. 1989

By this time, the Art of War is translated into thirteen different languages and becomes a major text source for MBA courses.

A.D. 1999

With increased interest in China, many scholars and authors write many different kinds of books about Sun Tzu and his Art of War. These all become very popular.

A.D. 2003

Tuttle Publishing published a book about Sun Tzu's Art of War as applied to negotiating in China, called *When Yes Means No* (see above). It becomes an immediate bestseller among businessmen negotiating contracts in China.

Appendix II

Sun Tzu's Most Famous Lesson

Sun Tzu's Opportunity

According to ancient Chinese history, the generals of Wu wanted to attack the Kingdom of Chu, but no action was taken, because of the inability of the generals to reach a clear plan in their strategic planning sessions. Wu Tzu Hsu and Po His spoke with each other: "We nurture officers and make plans on behalf of the King. These strategies will be advantageous to the State, and for this reason the King should attack Chu. But he has put off issuing the orders and does not have any intention to mobilize the army. What should we do?"

After a while the King of Wu got out of his bed, which was full of concubines, and summoned Wu Tzu Hsu and Po His before him. The king inquired, "I want to send forth the army. What do you think?" Wu Tzu Hsu and Po His replied: "Good idea! We would like to receive the order."

The King of Wu secretly thought the two of them harbored great enmity for Chu. He was deeply afraid that they would take the army out, act in a rash manner, only to be exterminated by the more powerful Chu. In meditative thought, the King mounted his tower, turned toward the southern wing, and groaned. After a while, he sighed. Finally, he burped. Only then did he light a cigarette. None of his ministers understood the King's thoughts. Wu Tzu Hsu secretly realized to himself that the King was not capable of making a decision. Seeing in the King's indecisiveness the necessity of a good corporate headquarters executive, he recommended Sun Tzu to him, the same way MBA programs would do to executives in the years to come.

Sun Tzu's Enlightenment

Sun Tzu, whose name was Wu, was a native of Wu. In the old days everybody in the village had the same name because they came from the same ancestral lineage. This explains why in Chinese culture people pay so much respect to their ancestors and elders. It also explains why the Chinese are so friendly to each other and get along so well. It also explains why China needs strict birth control measures.

Sun Tzu excelled at military strategy but dwelled in secrecy far away from civilization. Ordinary people did not know of his ability. This was good because Sun Tzu could work on his book secretly without fear of copyright infringement.

Wu Tzu Hsu, himself enlightened, wise, and skilled in discrimination, knew Sun Tzu could penetrate and destroy the enemy. One morning when he was discussing military affairs, he recommended Sun Tzu seven times. The King of Wu said. "Since you have found an excuse to advance this guy, I want to have him brought in." He questioned Sun Tzu about military strategy, and each time that Sun Tzu laid out a section of his book the King could not praise him enough, and soon requested the publishing rights.

Greatly pleased, the King of Wu inquired, "If possible, I would like a minor test of your military strategy."

Sun Tzu replied, "All things are possible. We can conduct a minor test with women from the inner palace."

The King said, "I agree."

Sun Tzu's Lesson

Sun Tzu said, "I would like to have two of your Majesty's beloved concubines act as company commanders, each to direct a company."

He then ordered all 300 women to wear helmets and armour, to carry swords and shields, and to stand. He instructed them in military methods, that in accord with the drum they should advance, withdraw, go left or right, or turn around. He had them know the prohibitions and then orders. "At the first beating of the drum you should all assemble, at the second drumming you should advance with your weapons, and at the third deploy into military formation." At the palace, women all covered their mouths and laughed.

Sun Tzu then personally took up the sticks and beat the drums, giving the orders three times and explaining them five times. They laughed as before. Sun Tzu saw that the women laughed continuously and would not stop.

Sun Tzu was enraged. He said to the Master of Laws, "Get the executioner's axe."

Sun Tzu then said, "If the instructions are not clear, if the explanations and orders are not trusted, it is the general's offense. When they have already been instructed three times and the orders explained five times, if the troops still do not perform, it is the fault of the officers. According to the rescripts for military discipline, what is the procedure?"

The Master of Laws said, "Decapitation!"

Sun Tzu then ordered the beheading of the two company commanders, the King's favourite concubines.

The King of Wu ascended his platform to observe just when they were about to behead his beloved concubines. He had an official hasten down to them with orders to say, "I already know the general is able to command forces. Without these two concubines, my food will not be sweet. It would not be appropriate to behead them."

Sun Tzu said, "I have already received my commission as commanding general. According to the rules for generals, when I, as a general, am in command of the army, even though you issue orders to me, I do not have to accept them? He then had the two women beheaded.

He again beat the drum, and the army of concubines went left and right, advanced and withdrew, and turned around in accordance with the prescribed standards, without daring to blink an eye. The two companies were silent, not daring to look around. Thereupon Sun Tzu reported to the King of Wu: "The army is already well-ordered. I would like Your Majesty to observe them. However you might want to employ them, even sending them forth into fire and water, will not present any difficulty. They can be used to settle 'All under Heaven.'"

The moral of this story: Sun Tzu's Art of War may also be used effectively in concubine management. For many doing business in China today, this may prove invaluable.

Glossary

Management Consultant
Somebody who takes the Rolex watch off your wrist in order to tell you the time, and then charges you the price of the watch.

Clerk
An over-booked law student training in a law firm and doing all the work which the lawyers charge for.

Lawyer
A glorified clerk. Someone you bring to the negotiation table when you have decided that you really do not want to do the deal, and need a reason to make it fall apart.

Prostitute
They do not exist in the People's Republic of China as prostitution was eliminated entirely along with other social evils of capitalism with the liberation of China in 1949. Not to be confused with a lawyer.

Tax Accountant

A moralist to whom you pay a lot of money so as to ensure that you will pay even more money in connection with every possible tax which could ever be imposed upon you in any form whatsoever.

Spratly Islands

A vast collection of rock islets in the South China Sea, currently under proposal before the Chinese government to be designated as a special China tax haven (in the tradition of the British Virgin and Cayman Islands) so as to facilitate the placing of all foreign lawyers and accountants working in China on these islets. The Spratleys are currently under dispute between the Chinese and Vietnamese governments, as the Vietnamese have the exact same idea.

Friendly Attitude

Agreeing immediately to all of the terms put forward by the Chinese side.

Unfriendly Attitude

Disagreeing with any one of the terms put forward by the Chinese side.

Letter of Intent

A non-legally binding legal document which sets forth the principles of friendship and mutual understanding which will become the subject of future argumentation over the misunderstandings which will definitely arise at the later stages of contract negotiation resulting from the assumed mutual understandings.

Joint Venture Contract

A legally binding document which overrides the principles of friendliness and mutual understanding set forth in the letter of intent and which legally documents most unfriendly discussions the issues for which mutual understanding has not been reached as well as the methods for resolving disputes which will inevitably arise from such misunderstandings.

Friendly Negotiations

This term must be included in every contract or agreement in China in order for it to be legally binding.

Mutual Understanding

The one term in the Chinese language most often quoted in negotiations and most often used out of context.

US Trade Representatve

For the Chinese, a most "unfriendly" negotiator. Someone with whom it is difficult to achieve "mutual understanding."